The Blended Family

Trust in the Lord with all your heart,
and lean not to your own understanding;
In all your ways acknowledge Him
and He shall direct your paths.
Proverbs 3:5–6

The Blended Family

Achieving Peace & Harmony in the Christian Home

Edward & Sharon Douglas

PROVIDENCE HOUSE PUBLISHERS
Franklin, Tennessee

Printed in the United States of America

04   03   02   01   00   1   2   3   4   5

Library of Congress Catalog Card Number: 00-100573

ISBN: 1-57736-179-2

Cover design by Gary Bozeman

Cover photo © 1999—www.arttoday.com

Unless otherwise indicated, Scripture quotations in this book are taken from the Holy Bible, the New King James Version, copyright 1982 by Thomas Nelson, Inc., and from the Woman's Study Bible, copyright 1995 by Thomas Nelson, Inc.

Verses marked NIV are taken from the New International Version. Trademarks are registered in the United States Patent and Trademark Office by International Bible Society.

PROVIDENCE HOUSE PUBLISHERS
238 Seaboard Lane • Franklin, Tennessee 37067
800-321-5692
www.providencehouse.com

To our children

Stacy, Kelly, Julius, Monica, Aaron, and Taylor

whom we love very dearly.
You are truly gifts from God.

Contents

Acknowledgments

We would like to thank Greg and Wanda Hunter, Erving and Wanda Williams, Eugene and Valerie Samuels, Michael and Sheila Woodson, Angela Corley, Calvin and Carolyn Parker, and most of all our family for their encouragement and support.

Our thanks go to dear friends Lawrence and Mary Davis for their spiritual support and friendship.

We would like to thank our support group of blended families who were open in sharing their experiences.

A special thank-you goes to Edward's Brothers-in-Disciplesip and facilitators, who have been instrumental in his spiritual growth and development.

We thank our mother Serena Hunter, who through her godly wisdom believed in what we were trying to accomplish. Our thanks go in loving memory to our deceased parents Robert and Margaret Douglas and Solomon Hunter, who instilled in us strong family values and taught us lifelong lessons.

We would like to thank our pastor and the Married Couples Ministry at our church, whose ministries have strengthened our marriage.

We would like to thank the Providence House family, particularly Marilyn Friedlander, Steven James, Kelly Bainbridge, Kelli Allen, and Elaine Wilson for their encouragement and assistance.

Introduction

John and Kathy were elated after their honeymoon. They could hardly wait to move into their new home with Kathy's two young children and John's two adolescent children. Kathy, thirty, lost her husband in a tragic car accident, and John, thirty-eight, lost his wife to leukemia.

John and Kathy met three years ago at a bereavement support group. They shared similar interests while spending time together at these sessions. Soon, they began dating, fell in love, and decided to get married. John and Kathy enjoyed their time together as a couple, but they did not feel it was necessary to share their time together with the children. "We love children, kids are not a problem," they both expressed to each other on more than one occasion.

As John and Kathy grew closer and their discussions centered around marriage and family, they thought it would be practical to spend more time with the children so that they could all get to know each other. Spending time together as a family would make the adjustment and transition into the new family structure easier for everyone. Although their ages were drastically different, the kids appeared to get along well together during the times they were together alone. John's kids enjoyed having a younger brother and sister.

John and Kathy married. Their wedding was a grand occasion. The children and their families were very happy for them. Three months after the marriage, Kathy confided in her closest friend:

I don't care for his kids. He spends our money on his kids and questions me when I need money for my kids. His former in-laws and mine call our home and influence the kids to do things that we are uncomfortable with. The kids don't respect us because we won't give in to these ideas and suggestions of their relatives. John is so hard on Keith and Erica, and when I complain, he tells me that they have no structure or limitations and that I spoiled them. I feel he spoils his children. They get everything they ask for. The kids sense the conflict between us, and they appear to be confused and unhappy. Well, what do most kids do when there is a conflict between parents, they play one against the other.

My children have lost their privacy. They had their own rooms and now they have to share their rooms with stepsiblings. Needless to say, this situation creates many fights. I am so confused. Am I supposed to love his kids and should he love my children? I don't love his kids. As a matter of fact, I don't even like them at times. Well, maybe I like them. These issues are creating conflict in our marriage. I thought this relationship would work, but I don't know if it will last a year.

Many couples share the same bewilderment that John and Kathy experienced in their newly created family structure. The issues in John and Kathy's family and in other blended families are significantly more complex than issues in traditional families. Issues in blended families may be similar to John and Kathy's or they may be quite different.

Our intent in this book is to discuss biblical solutions to the complex issues that a large number of blended families experience. It is our sincere hope that this book will lead couples to achieve a more peaceful and harmonious blended family. This book is not intended to be a how-to guide for those who are contemplating divorce and remarriage. Rather, it is a guide for those who have learned a valuable lesson from past mistakes. Traditional families may also benefit from this book by applying the principles shared in support of couples keeping the marriage covenant.

Our Personal Story

Shortly after Edward and I married, we began to face the reality of combining two families into a single household. As we faced this challenge and the realization that the issues were putting a strain on our marriage, we decided divorce was not and never would be an option. We were both divorced before we remarried. We decided that we love each other and we would commit to work on building our

relationship with the Lord and with each other. We prayed that God would give us the wisdom and guidance to effectively handle the issues in our family.

We experienced feelings similar to those of John and Kathy. We also realized immediately that blending a family was not as easy as it appeared in the joyous Brady family on the television show, *The Brady Bunch*. We expected our blended family to function like a traditional family. How could I feel this way when I rationalized that my children had a father who fulfilled the role of father in their lives, and that they did not really need another father? I believed that it was not necessary for Edward to step into my life and be a father to my children by taking on the duties and responsibilities of fatherhood. He felt the same about my relationship with his daughters. Needless to say, this understanding between the two of us created problems.

Issues

As we continued to struggle through issues, we decided we could possibly find solutions to our problems by reading books about stepfamilies. We also sought advice from other couples in blended families. We could not find the answers we were looking for. We found that our cultural traditions and resources focus primarily on first-marriage traditional families and that resources we read on stepfamilies were written from a psychological point of view by psychologists who were not in stepfamilies.

We continued to struggle with issues, and the stress and dilemma of these complex family issues led us to make the best decision of our lives: We accepted Jesus Christ as our personal savior and joined a local church. We had considered ourselves Christians because of our beliefs. We were both brought up in the church as children, but like many, we strayed in pursuit of worldly happiness. Praying, studying, meditating on, and discussing the Word of God became part of our lives. We attended Christian seminars, formal classes, weekend marriage retreats, and began reading spiritual books about marriage. We immediately experienced changes in our relationship with the Lord and with each other.

We strongly believe that reading and applying the Word of God to our marriage allowed us to put behind the guilt, bitterness, and pain of divorce. It also allowed us to apply the same love God has for us to each other and to our children. We believe there are no issues that we are faced with in this world today that are not addressed in Scripture, and the Holy Bible is our guide for living. The answers to all our concerns are in the Word of God.

Even though our marriage was strengthened by applying the principles we learned, we continued to face the challenges unique to the blended family. These challenges continued until a traumatic incident occurred which led us to cry out to the Lord, and we began our spiritual search for answers. The following account is what led to writing this book.

We have six children. My husband has two biological children ages twenty-nine and twenty-six who never lived in our family home. I have three children ages sixteen, fourteen, and eleven who live in our home. Together, we have a four-year-old daughter.

One evening, my fourteen-year-old, upset over the fact that I was going to discipline her by taking away her stereo for two weeks, created an explosive situation between the two of us. She attempted to take the stereo away from me while we both were walking down the steps. After we struggled in anger for control of the stereo, she called my former spouse to ask if he could pick her up at our home. She yelled, "I don't want to live here anymore. I'm going to live with my father." My former spouse picked her up from our home.

The next day the worse nightmare of my life began; I received a call from Child Protective Services. My former spouse accused me of physically, mentally, and emotionally abusing our child. I was devastated. "Not me," I said. "Why would he do this to me?" I asked myself. "He did not call our home to even ask me what happened." Everyone knows how I am with my children, neighbors, friends, even coworkers. People I confided in could only make the statement, "He knows better!" In addition, my children do not exhibit the behavior of mentally or emotionally abused children. Our fourteen-year-old is a very good child and always attempts to make the right choices. This incident was an isolated incident and there was no need for this situation to be blown out of proportion. I began praying, "Lord you know I love my children very much. I have been through many things in my life, but this, how can I handle this?" I continued to pray, "Lord, you know my heart, you know about the unselfish sacrifices I have made for my children."

We could not sleep that evening. I sat up and could only stare blankly at the wall. We felt our family would never be the same again.

The next day we met with Child Protective Services. The investigator had already met with our daughter and her father. She concluded after the investigation that this was not a case of abuse and decided there was no reason to write a report. The investigator strongly recommended that my former spouse withdraw his complaint from the court. He withdrew the complaint and the case was dismissed. We thanked God and thought to ourselves, when is this madness going to end? Again, reality hit us: We are not like the traditional family. Outside influences can have a devastating impact on the blended family. (This statement is not intended to discourage parents from filing a complaint if a parent feels there is a legitimate concern about abuse of a child.) I felt that my family and I were being controlled by my ex who refuses to follow court-order custody and visitation agreements. I have custody of the children; however, he feels that since his children live in our home, he has the right as their father to do whatever he wants to do. All attempts to work out a cordial relationship on behalf of the children have proven impossible.

One day, while sitting at my desk at work still stressed out, I pondered over the situation and again communicated with the Lord. "Lord, please give me the strength to handle these issues. Lord, you want families to build their homes on a solid foundation. Lord, my husband is the head of our home, and there should be only one head. Lord, you want parents to raise, teach, and discipline children according to your Word. How can we do this, when we have outside influences that interfere with the leadership in the home?" The verses started to come to mind. It was as if the Holy Spirit was guiding me:

The Lord provides a way of escape out of any situation you are in only if you seek him. The Lord will fight your battles. *Trust in the Lord with all your heart, lean not to your own understanding. In all thy ways acknowledge Him and He shall direct your paths* (Prov. 3:5–6).

I hung on these verses, discussed my thoughts with Edward, and we began our search for the answers.

As revealed above, there are barriers to living in harmony in the blended family. This book will address the hurt and pain of past relationships, whether losing a loved one or experiencing the pain of divorce. We will discuss God's perfect plan for marriage and building character later in the book. We also discuss the awesome responsibility God places on parents to raise His children. Finally, we discuss scriptural solutions to the challenging issues in blended families. We want the reader to gain a clear understanding of the issues and biblical solutions to blending families. By applying the Word of God to your marriage and family, you will acquire the necessary tools to defeat the enemy and build your home on a solid biblical foundation.

We found countless stories in the Bible of what we today call blended or stepfamilies. These families were referred to as extended families in the Bible. For example, Moses was adopted by Pharaoh's daughter, who had compassion for him (Exod. 2:10). Moses was raised by Pharaoh, and he called him son. In the story of Ruth, Ruth and Boaz cared for Naomi, who was Ruth's mother-in-law from her first marriage. Abraham's family was a blended family (Gen. 16) (Gen. 17:23, 27).

Issues in life will surface which will lead us to seek answers by studying the Word of God. The Bible is our blueprint for how we are to live our lives. We want to share what we have learned with others who are in traditional as well as in blended families. We love the Lord and realize that applying the Word of God to our marriage and to raising our children has truly led to a happier and more fulfilling family life.

Chapter 1

Blending Is Not Easy

"So Abram said to Lot, 'Please Let there be no strife between you and me, and between my herdsmen and your herdsmen; for we are brethren.'"
—Genesis 13:8

The initial blending of families can be visualized by thinking of what it is like bringing together furniture from two different households into your new home. After the furniture is placed, you realize it just doesn't match, or it doesn't quite fit. You spend time and energy arranging and rearranging the furniture to try to get the best blend without offending anyone. Similarly, when a number of persons of varying ages and stages of development suddenly come together from different family households with different traditions from previous families, problems will likely occur. It is often difficult to reach an agreement on how to handle problems, especially if the couple did not discuss potential problems before the marriage.

While all families face pressures from time to time, the blended family is often faced with an extremely complex set of relationships that create additional problems and pressures for the family. Unexpected issues surface concerning discipline, finances, outside influences, invasion of privacy, and so on that are often difficult to resolve. Roles can become very confusing, especially to parents and children. The family is not prepared for the stress and anxiety that suddenly appears. Former relationships with family members and friends often become clouded. Many of these difficulties and the frustration over the inability to resolve these issues are what lead to divorce and the ultimate breakup of the family unit.

The blended family or stepfamily is very common today. According to U.S. census figures, about 70 percent of stepfamilies dissolve within ten years. Couples in blended families divorce at a higher rate than those in traditional marriages. Statistics reveal that 50 percent of first marriages fail, while 70 percent of second marriages end in divorce. It is noted that arguments about children are the main factor in the breakup of second marriages. "Based on the National Center for Health Statistics 1997 provisional statistical report on divorce there are 1,163,000 divorces annually

1

and the likelihood of remarriages ending in divorce is 60 percent."[1] The divorce rate continues to escalate. The National Center for Health Statistics also reports that the number of stepfamilies increased 36 percent from 1980 to 1990 and the number is still increasing. The U.S. Census Bureau reports one out of every three Americans is now a stepparent, stepchild, stepsibling, or some other member of a stepfamily. Twenty-one percent of all married couples with dependent children now contain at least one stepparent, and 7.3 million children are in stepfamilies.

Not only are couples in blended families divorcing at a high rate, but it appears couples in traditional marriages are also divorcing at a high rate as well.

Worldwide, divorce rates increased over most of the past fifty years and reached a high of 50 percent in 1980 and has hovered near or at that level ever since. Man-made laws that had preserved a vast number of troubled marriages by permitting divorce only on proof of serious spousal misconduct gave way in the 1970's to "no-fault" laws that granted divorce simply on the assertion of incompatibility. There was a sudden increase in the number of divorces.[2]

The divorce rate in the United States will probably continue to remain high because of another historical trend: married couples today are less likely than their counterparts in earlier cohorts to consider their marriages very happy.[3]

Can you imagine Satan in his attempt to destroy marriages slipping into those laws and coining the phrase incompatibility? Slight differences or conflict would suggest to a couple that they are incompatible and would make them less likely to want to work things out. In fact, we heard recently on a local radio station that there are so many divorces in this country that some states are considering changing divorce laws to make it more difficult to obtain a divorce. With so many divorces being granted based solely on incompatibility, it is no wonder the divorce rate is so high.

After God had created the heavens and the earth and all that was upon it, He saw that Adam was alone. "Then the Lord God said, it is not good for the man to be alone, I will make him a helper suitable or fit for him." When God made Adam, he made Adam in his image and he made Eve a helper comparable to Adam (Gen. 2:18). Webster's dictionary defines comparable as "similar or equal to. Suitable means fitting, appropriate."[4] Man was created in the image of God. He created them male and female in the image of God (Gen. 1:26–27). Although there are physical differences, husbands and wives were created as coequals to carry out different roles. "The woman was designed as the perfect counter part for the man, the woman was neither inferior nor superior, but she was alike and equal to man in her person hood while different and unique in her function."[5] God gave Adam an agenda or plan and Eve was to help him carry it out. God made Eve from Adam's side. They were made from the same; therefore, they were more alike than they were different. Eve was created to be perfectly suited for Adam. This marriage was to be perfect in its establishment: one man and one woman in a lifetime commitment.

As a result of sin, Adam and Eve were cursed for their disobedience. As a result of the fall, the fellowship with God was broken, man and woman became alienated, pain was added to childbirth, tyranny and abuse to headship, and rebellion to submission.[6] One curse was that there would be a conflict of power and control between the husband and wife. Gen. 3:16 states one of the curses on Eve: "Your desire shall be for your husband, and he shall rule over you." Eve's desire would be to dominate Adam as Adam attempts to have power over her. "Woman would have a sin tendency to disrespect man's role of leadership, and man in his sinfulness would tend to abuse his authority and abandoned his responsibility for leadership."[7] There was harmony and peace between Adam and Eve before sin, but they chose to ignore the Creator's plan and do things their own way. Conflict and friction squashed any attempts for a peaceful union. However, thank God that He sent His only begotten son, Jesus Christ, who came to redeem us; therefore, couples can work towards harmony and peace in the family.

Why Blending a Family Is So Difficult

Blending is not easy because the remarried couple brings into the newly created family unrealistic expectations about the family's future. The family must also accomplish the task of becoming like the traditional family. Before the marriage, the couple's belief is that the children will welcome this wonderful new person entering their lives. The family is not prepared for the stress and anxiety that suddenly appears. Blended families are often reminded that they are in a blended family when questions arise about the children. For example, when asked, "How many children do you have?" the couple stumbles over answers like, "We have seven" (which includes all the children), or "She has four and I have three." Couples have a tendency to forget and may not include the children that are not living in the home, especially if these children never lived in the home.

Born of conflict and loss, new-found commitment, and often heart-wrenching transition, these families confront myriad lifestyle adjustments and challenges. Children usually suffer the most in blended families. Children of stepfamilies face a higher risk of emotional and behavioral problems and are less likely to be resilient in stressful situations.

Based on many large-scale surveys that compare various family structures, children living with both biological parents tend to fare best having fewer physical, emotional or learning difficulties from infancy throughout childhood than do children in other family structures. Adolescents are less likely to use drugs and more likely to graduate from high school. In adulthood, they are more likely to graduate from college and continue to develop with self-confidence, social acceptance and career success.[8]

"The reasons are that both parents have known and loved the child since birth. Couples compensate for each other's shortcomings and enhance each other's strengths."[9]

Within the blended family, the stepchild's life is profoundly altered. While new partners are initially likely to be happy with the remarriage, this may not be the case for the children who must suddenly negotiate a new set of family relationships not only with a stepparent but often also with stepsiblings, stepgrandparents and so on, most of whom they would not have chosen on their own.

As a result of the stress of handling the children within the family, parents

3

often become frustrated, protective, and noncommunicable. The reason for this is the lack of immediate commitment to bond with the stepchild. Bonding is not instant. It often takes time to bond with children depending on the ages and personalities of the individual child. It may take longer to bond with some children because of unresolved anger and their loyalty to biological parents. Parents must work towards developing a relationship with the children.

Edward and I had no idea that blending two families would cause such turmoil. There were so many complex issues that we had never given any thought to before the marriage. We were confronted with many challenges that we did not experience in our previous marriages. Edward had two young adult daughters whom I had a difficult time bonding with. I was experienced at raising young children, and I had no idea how to be stepmother to young adults I barely knew. I wrestled with what role I should play in their lives. Should I be a friend, mother, and nurturer to these children who lived in their own homes?

In an attempt to develop a relationship with his youngest daughter, I initially became very overbearing. This was not an attempt to make her like me because I knew I was a likeable caring person, but it was to help her get through tough decisions she was having difficulty with during this time in her life. She welcomed the relationship, and in a short period of time it developed into a cordial and respectful firendship. She soon became very distant, however, and I believe this was because of her loyalty to her own biological mother and because of her uncertainty of what her role should be in the family. Edward's oldest daughter has yet to acknowledge her new extended family and half sister and has

no contact with anyone except her father. We pray that one day she will acknowledge that we all love and care for her.

My children visited my former spouse every weekend while we were dating, and we did not spend a great deal of time with them. I remember thinking the same thoughts John and Kathy had. We truly believed it did not matter whether we spent a great deal of time with the children. We, too, felt we basically liked children. We had a great time together and we loved each other and at the time this was all that really mattered.

Before we married, Edward thought it would be a great idea to take my kids to an amusement park. They were very young at the time and of course they were excited about going to an amusement park. This was our way in this short period of time to begin developing a relationship between Edward and the kids. He had been in their company on only a few occasions. They had fun with him during those times, and he liked them. Well, we went to the amusement park and had a great time. On the way home, my young, inquisitive, delightful children did everything except kick him out of the car. Needless to say, I was embarrassed, but I rationalized to myself, "They are just being kids." On the other hand, Edward thought to himself "These kids have no discipline, a firm disciplinarian is what they need." Shortly after this experience, we made plans to be married.

Blending is inherently very difficult. It takes time for families to develop their own history and traditions. It takes time for spouses to organize themselves as parents of infants, toddlers, school-age children, adolescents, and adult children. At the same time, it takes time for children to organize themselves as siblings and stepchildren.

A blended family may consist of stepchildren or extended-family members such as grandparents, in-laws, cousins, aunts, uncles, and other relatives who live in the same household. A blended family can be formed when a single-parent or widow (or widower) with or without children marries someone with children. A traditional family may become a blended family if an adopted or foster child is brought into the family structure. For the purpose of this book, we will focus on blended families, which are formed when a widow (widower), divorcée (divorcé), or single parent marries another person with children.

As this new family form continues to become more prevalent, it is important to become aware of the traps and pitfalls unique to the blended family. Researchers indicate blended families report that nothing feels quite right and that blending two families is an inherently disorganizing experience.

Even in the best of circumstances, harmony takes time to achieve. The blended family's goal must be to strengthen the family which starts with first strengthening the marital bond. This can be accomplished by studying God's plan for marriage and then growing spiritually as a family unit. This will ultimately lead to peace, harmony, and contentment within the family. A peace that you never thought could exist. There is no magic formula but faith in God, prayer, and studying and applying the Word of God to your life. We still have our challenges, but we have learned to pray for guidance.

Dealing with the issues in the blended family begins with: (1) healing from divorce, admitting sins, and asking for forgiveness; (2) understanding God's perfect plan for marriage; and (3) building character within ourselves so that we are able to face the challenges in the blended family.

King David was a guy with family problems as well as spiritual ups and downs. When he or his children sinned, they inevitably reaped the consequences of their wrong choices. David experienced God's love, grace, and forgiveness often enough that he felt confident in his prayers. He boldly asked God to bless his family.

Chapter 2

Surrendering to God

Then He Said, "To what shall we liken the Kingdom of God? Or with what parable shall we picture it? It is like a mustard seed which, when it is sown on the ground, is smaller than all the seeds on the earth; but when it is sown, it grows up and becomes greater than all herbs, and shoots out large branches, so that the birds of the air may nest under its shade." —Mark 4:30–32

Before you begin to receive healing and the spiritual blessings God will provide to your family, you must first accept Jesus Christ as your personal savior.

Salvation requires not only God's initial action but also your response. There are three aspects of God's salvation or deliverance: justification, sanctification and glorification. Justification is God's deliverance from sin's penalty. When a person accepts Christ he or she becomes totally free from the penalty of sin and spiritual death (Rom. 3:23–25).

Sanctification is God's progressive deliverance of a believer from sin's power (Eph. 5:26). God's desire is that the believer mature and become Christ like. God has given the Holy Spirit to aid believers in the process of sanctification. Glorification is God's ultimate deliverance of a believer from sin's power. When the Lord returns for his children (1 Cor. 15:51–57), you must surrender yourself to the Lord; at this point salvation has occurred. The power of Christ in the believer is greater than the power of sin over that believer (2 Tim. 1:12). Christ covers your sin.[1]

Sin separates man from God. Jesus Christ is God's only provision for man's sin.

Jesus said to him "I am the way, and the truth, and the life. No one comes to the Father, except through Me." (John 14:6)

Jesus came upon this earth to die for our sins. Through his death and resurrection, Jesus enables each of us to receive eternal life. He wants to be your Lord and Savior.

Receiving Christ involves turning to God from self (repentance) and trusting Christ to come into our lives to forgive our sins and to make us the kind of people He wants us to be. Just to agree intellectually that Jesus Christ is the Son of God and that He died on the cross for our sins is not enough. Nor is it enough to have an emotional experience. We receive Jesus Christ by faith as an act of the will.[2]

Pray and ask God to have mercy on your soul, confess your sins and ask God's forgiveness, ask Him to fill you with the Holy Spirit, submit yourself to his will, pray, and study the Word of God.

Spiritual growth requires the study of God's word. Growth requires letting the Word of God dwell in your heart and soul. The Bible is the inspired Word of God, and you can live an abundant life by drawing on the Scriptures and teachings of the Word of God. The more we read and meditate on the Word of God and allow the Holy Spirit to dwell within us, the more fruitful we become.

"My son, do not forget my law, But let your heart keep my commands; For length of days and long life And peace they will add to you. Let not mercy and truth forsake you; bind them around your neck, write them on your tablet of your heart, And so find favor and high esteem in the sight of God and man" (Proverbs 3:1–4).

Surrendering to the will of God requires us to put on the whole armor of God to stand against the wiles of the devil (Eph. 6:11–18). So many of us learn this valuable lesson too late. We use our own minds to solve the storms in life, which ultimately leads to confusion and unhappiness.

Our theme of this book is based on the Scripture Proverbs 3:5–6.

We must therefore *trust in the Lord with all our hearts;* we must believe that he is able to do what he will, wise to do what is best, and good, according to his promise, to do what is best for us, if we love him and serve him. We must, with an entire submission and satisfaction, depend upon him to perform all things for us, *and*

not lean to our own understanding, as if we could, by any forecast of our own, without God, help ourselves, and bring our affairs to a good issue. Those who know themselves cannot but find their own understanding to be a broken reed, which, if they lean to, will certainly fail them. In all our conduct we must be confident of God's wisdom, power, and goodness. By prayer *in all your ways acknowledge God. . . .* We must ask his advice and beg direction from him in every situation. We must ask success of him as those who know the race is not to the swift. We must refer ourselves to him as one from whom our judgment proceeds, and patiently and wait his award. In everything make our requests known. . . . *He shall direct thy paths* so that thy way shall be safe

---

Live a Spirit-Controlled Life

Faith (trust in God and His promises) is the only means by which a Christian can live a spirit-controlled life. As you continue to trust Christ moment by moment:

1. Your life will demonstrate more and more of the fruit of the spirit (Gal. 5:22–23); and will be more and more conformed to the image of Christ (Rom. 12:2; 2 Cor. 3:18).

2. Your prayer life and study of God's Word will become more meaningful.

3. You will experience His power in witnessing (Acts 1:8).

4. You will be prepared for spiritual conflict against the world (1 John 2:1–17); against the flesh (Gal. 5:16–17); and against Satan (1 Pet. 5:7–9; Eph. 6:10–13).

5. You will experience His power to resist temptation and sin (1 Cor. 10:13; Phil. 4:13; Eph. 1:19–23; 6:10; 2 Tim. 1:7; Rom. 6: 1–16).[3]

and good and the issue happy at last. Put yourselves totally under divine guidance.[4]

Finally, the closer couples get to God, the closer they become to each other. The closer couples are to God, the more focused they become on their roles as husband, wife, and parents. The closer couples get to God, the less selfishness will be visible in their character. The closer couples get to God, the more they experience the peace, harmony, and happiness they desire.

Our relationship truly began to heal and change when we surrendered to God's will. As we became stronger and experienced changes in our relationship and family, we were able to witness to other married couples the amazing power of healing in marriage and family. We listen to people complain about their problems, and the only direction we can give them is towards the Word of God.

Scottish writer and pastor Thomas Cuthris wrote:

The Bible is an armory of heavenly weapons, a laboratory of infallible medicines, a mine of exhaustless wealth. It is a guidebook for every road, a chart for every sea, a medicine for every malady, a balm for every wound. Rob us of our Bible and our sky has lost its sun.

Chapter 3

Dealing with Loss

. . . The Lord has annointed Me . . . to comfort all who mourn, to give them beauty for ashes, the oil of joy for mourning, the garment of praise for the spirit of heaviness. . . . —Isaiah 61:2–3

Coping with the loss of a loved one through death, divorce, or separation is an overwhelmingly painful experience. It takes sometimes years to recover from the loss. Blended families must be aware that everyone in the family has experienced loss, and steps must be taken that will help each family member cope with feelings and heal from past experiences.

Feelings of disappointment and anger may surface in children who are suddenly forced to adjust to a new family after separating from their biological parent whom they deeply love and care for. Memories and fears may surface in couples who have baggage from a previous marriage or past relationship. This baggage may raise doubts about their ability to love and trust again. A widower or widow may question his or her ability to love again after the death of a spouse. A single parent may experience feelings similar to the divorcée who loses a loved one.

God is gracious, righteous, and compassionate. He cares about your heaviness, depression, pain, and hurt.

God will walk with you through whatever circumstances you encounter. Cry out to the Lord! God's understanding is unlimited. He knows what is best for you and He will heal your broken heart.

The loss of a special relationship is one of the deepest psychological losses experienced. Divorce, separation, death, or the loss of a special friendship is often heartbreaking and, if not addressed, can result in a poor self-image, feelings of rejection, betrayal, loss of hope, disruption in daily routines, and the loss of faith in God and mankind. Author and human development expert Donald Joy believes, "The best news of all is that many people who have been broken are now mended, and the grace of God is the glue."[1]

Divorce

Divorce is often accompanied by substantial physiological and psychological stress. The stress of divorce can

9

and often does result in social isolation, role overload, and financial hardship. Many divorcées experience self-pity, depression, guilt, and an uncertainty about the future. God, however, made Jesus Christ who knew no sin to be sin on our behalf that we might become the righteousness of God in Him. When our trust is in Jesus Christ our Savior and Lord, we are saved from sin. Our old self was crucified with Jesus Christ, that our body of sin might be done away with and rendered powerless. We should no longer be slaves to sin. (Rom. 6:6)

Pray that God heals you from the guilt and pain of the past. Do not beat yourself up about unpleasant past experiences and do not allow others to cause self-doubt. People will tend to remind you of past sins not necessarily by what they say but by their behavior and actions. Distance yourself from those who do not provide you with positive support and encouragement that you need to grow in Christ. Allow the Lord to strengthen you. Memorize this verse: "My flesh and my heart fail, but God is the strength of my heart and my portion forever" (Ps. 73:26).

Healing from the consequences of divorce begins with a clear understanding of what the Bible states about divorce.

It is important to repent and receive forgiveness of past sins (1 John 1:9), to forgive others, pray for healing from past wounds, forget the past (Phil. 3:13) and move on to the road of recovery (Phil. 3:13b–14). Healing takes place when anxieties and fears are dispelled. It sometimes takes longer than what we think to rid ourselves of these fears.[2]

God has always had one basic way of dealing with human failure. That is, to come alongside us with the gift of forgiveness and by his healing touch bring that possibility of health and growth.[3]

We forgive the adulterer in our churches much more quickly than we forgive the woman who has suffered the abandonment of divorce, or the man who has chosen to remarry. We welcome the converted murderer to our pulpits and lionize the reformed purveyor of smut. But somehow we feel it is only right that life-long suffering result for anyone who has been involved in any way in the one unforgivable sin of our day. How strange.[4]

Finally, identify your emotions and learn to channel them into positive behaviors. As painful memories surface, you can bring them to God for healing and restoration, allowing Him to remove the shame that has been linked to those memories.

Death of a Spouse

When a person loses someone through death, it is sometimes very difficult to recover. To some, the lost relationship is what made life worth living. As a result of the grief, some people experience the opposite of a healthy reaction. The bereaved are unable to cope. They tend to suffer the effects of the loss of their physical abilities, financial status, and their diminished circle of friends.

"In recent times, mourning has become a more private and less emotional affair. The bereft are often encouraged to 'bear up'; friends and relatives do less consoling and more advising them to keep busy, to remarry, and to look on the bright side."[5]

A grieving person can, with the presence of God's spirit within, gain strength in the soul, strength of faith, to serve God and to do His will. Where

His spirit dwells, there He dwells. With God's fullness, healing will occur and the needs of the faithful will be fulfilled.

The loss of a husband or a wife is a devastating experience. The widow and widower should be surrounded by people of faith. People who will provide comfort and encouragement. The widower must pray that the Lord will provide comfort, strength, and peace.

Single Parents

God is aware of the awesome challenge and responsibility of the unmarried single parent. Single parents experience similar hurt and pain when dealing with the loss of a previous relationship with the absent parent. The single parent must also face the challenges of raising a child alone. Single parents must work towards promoting a healthy Christian environment for both the child and themselves. Single parents are admonished to acknowledge the hurt and pain, confess sins, and forgive themselves and others. Most of all, they should not harbor bitterness. Bitterness keeps a person in bondage. Guilt and pain should be handled by following the above guidance to the divorced person. The single parent can be nurtured spiritually and emotionally by reading and studying the Word of God.

If the single parent is considering marriage, he or she should pray that God will send a faithful person that believes in God, is self-sacrificing, loves unconditionally, and is committed to the covenant of marriage. The single parent should also pray for a partner who is committed to training and raising godly children.

Whether married, divorced, single, or widowed, a person receives spiritual strength from knowing that Jesus enables one to do the work of the Lord in this world and to be happy regardless of one's circumstances.

Meditate on this Psalm of David:

I cried out to God with my voice, and he gave ear to me. In the day of my trouble I sought the Lord. My hand was stretched out in the night without ceasing; my soul refused to be comforted. I remembered God, and was troubled; I complained, and my spirit was overwhelmed. You hold my eyelids open; I am so troubled that I cannot speak. I have considered the days of old, the years of ancient times. I call to remembrance my song in the night; I meditate within my heart, and my spirit makes diligent search. (Ps. 77:1–6)

Chapter 4

Surviving Divorce and Remarriage

But did he not make them one, having a remnant of the Spirit? And why one? He seeks godly offspring. Therefore, take heed to your spirit, and let none deal treacherously with the wife of his youth. —Malachi 2:15

After three years of marriage, John and Kathy felt angry, hurt, and betrayed. They discussed divorce. Their fantasy of living happily ever after was slowly becoming a marriage filled with distress. The promise of security, happiness, and intimacy had faded away because of the magnitude of issues in their marriage. Not only were John, Kathy, and the children having a difficult time adjusting to each other, they were also having a difficult time healing from the grief and loss of past relationships. They argued about the children, finances, and about Kathy's former in-law's influence on her biological children. John did not feel he was getting the respect he deserved as the head of household.

Their children were experiencing the emotional pain of three years of trying to adjust to new stepparents and to stepsiblings while healing from the loss of their biological parents. The stress had led to anger, sadness, and isolation among everyone in the family, and there was no peace. To complicate matters even more, the children were not doing well in school. John and Kathy decided divorce was the only solution. After weeks of discussing divorce, they both decided this was not the best course of action. They still loved each other. Two weeks later, while John and Kathy were visiting friends, a Christian couple witnessed to them about how the Lord had blessed their marriage. They talked extensively with this couple who were also in a blended family. They were surprised the couple had similar issues but were able to overcome these issues by seeking God's direction. The couple prayed with them and John and Kathy decided to attend their local church. They also made an appointment to see a Christian counselor.

John and Kathy are not alone. The trauma of losing a loved one though separation, death, or divorce affects many lives.

Facts about Divorce and Remarriage

About 65 percent of remarriages involve children from the prior marriage and thus form a stepfamily or blended family. "One out of every three Americans is now a stepparent, stepchild, stepsibling or some other member of a stepfamily."[1] These are very astounding statistics.

Popular wisdom suggests there is no guarantee for either sex that love is better the second time around: remarried people generally report lower average rates of happiness than people in first marriages, and their divorce rate by age 50 is 20 percent higher.

One reason is that some lonely divorced people marry too quickly, on the rebound (sometimes to the first person who seems interested). In many instances, however, an important factor is the disruptive effects of stepchildren. For remarriages involving stepchildren, one study found the divorce rate within three years after marriage to be 17 percent, compared with 10 percent for childless remarriages and 6 percent for first-time marriages.

Other research confirms that stepchildren are a source of conflict between husband and wife but suggest that such conflict is lower in the early years of the marriage and is less likely to occur if the couple has a biological child of their own.

From one perspective, the high divorce rate of the remarried may mean that these individuals have learned from their first marriage experience and are quicker to recognize problems and thus are quicker to either resolve the conflict or sever the tie. That this may be the case is suggested by the fact that, compared with people in first marriages, remarried people are more likely to describe their marriages as either very happy or quite unhappy with less middle ground.[2]

Surviving divorce and remarriage requires accepting past sins, asking for forgiveness, and having a strong commitment to making the current marriage last till death do you part.

Feelings as a Result of Separation

When couples separate, they find that they have suddenly lost benefits they did not notice existed. Emotional dependence deepens over time even though couples may not realize it.

Former partners are often surprised by the currents of emotion that remain after the breakup. Hostile former partners often have to face rejection that is now unrestrained, while amicable former partners find that their attempts to start a new life are undermined by feelings of regret and doubt.

The longer the couples had been together, the more intimate they once were, and the more commitments they shared such as joint property, mutual friends and most importantly children, the more stress a breakup brings. There are two reasons for the unanticipated problems. First, before the breakup, unhappy partners are often focused on what is missing in their relationship that they are hardly aware of the needs currently being well served.

National surveys find that single divorced adults of every age are the least likely to be very happy with their lives not only when they are compared to married people but also when they are compared to never-married or widowed adults.[3]

There are lasting effects of divorce especially when children are involved. "The consequences are usually worse than either partner anticipated in almost every dimension—health, happiness, self-esteem, financial stability, social interaction, and child-rearing."[4] Children are often confused and emotionally affected by arbitrary divorces. The situation gets even more complicated with remarriage. Overall, the vast majority of stepchildren—70 percent—are fairly well adjusted, cautions James Bray, a psychologist with the Baylor College of Medicine, Houston. Still, in his nine-year study for the National Institutes of Health, of 198 step and traditional families, he found that 20–30 percent of stepchildren have significant behavior problems, while 10–15 percent of those in traditional families do.

From Prince and Princess to Tiger and Tigress—The Reality of Expectations

Why do couples divorce? Why do people have such a difficult time getting along? Couples feel in love when they meet and while they are dating. They take off in this fantasy consumed by the expectation that everything will be perfect. You remember those mushy feelings of infatuation, the sleepless nights and dreaming about this wonderful person in your life. What happens? Surprisingly,

Psychologists believe that an underlying explanation for the increasing divorce rate is a shift that has led most spouses today to expect a great deal more from each other than spouses in the past did. In past marriages, as long as both partners did their jobs, the marriage usually survived. Husbands and wives of the past usually did not expect to really understand each other: they generally assumed that masculinity and femininity are opposites and that the sexes therefore are naturally a mystery to each other. Our expectations have elevated compared to years ago. Marriage partners have a much more flexible view of marriage roles and responsibilities and are likely to expect each other to be a friend, lover, confidant, as well as wage earner, and caregiver. While couples expect more from a relationship than couples once did, they may at the same time devote less of themselves to a marriage.

The solution to this dilemma is not to raise expectations for oneself but to raise expectations of oneself, replacing the unfettered pursuit of self-interest with a willingness to commit fully to the marriage and make the sacrifices and investments needed to make it succeed.[5]

A couple's concept of marriage can be distorted by unrealistic unmet expectations and fantasy images of marriage which are worldly views of how marriage should be. Suddenly, you hit reality and disenchantment after your fantasy images dissolve and you wonder what went wrong. It appears from various opinions about why people divorce that the cycle appears to be: fantasy, infatuation, reality, and then disenchantment. Webster's definition of fantasy is "a more or less connected series of mental images, as in a daydream usually involving some unfulfilled desire; a portrayal of highly imaginative characters or settings that have no counterparts in the real world." Infatuation is defined as the state of being "inspired with foolish or

14

shallow love or affection" and reality is "the quality of being true to life."

Reality sets in when the fantasy or infatuation dissolves. Many people are surprised when this feeling sets in. Disillusionment or disenchantment leads to anger, blame, selfishness, isolation, and a feeling of being "turned off" and a lack of desire to communicate. These feelings eventually lead to unhappiness, stress, depression, and ultimately separation and divorce. It is a condition of being all alone even though you are married.

To overcome disillusionment, understand that unrealistic expectations were created by a distorted worldly view of how marriage should be. The worldly view of marriage is based on the feeling that our spouse should be everything to us and that our spouse has the responsibility to make us feel happy. This view further implies that couples are happy always, every day, void of serious problems and issues. When problems arise and they are too much to handle, couples are encouraged to do what makes them happy, that is, leave and find someone else.

Most people believe their marriage can burn out and that people change and this change brings about the desire to experience different and exciting things. Our society promotes change and personal growth, which most people believe contribute to self-fulfillment. Therefore, it is conceivable why couples grow apart and let go of a marriage that is no longer fulfilling. Some couples feel that letting go is a personal triumph. Have you ever heard words from people who are having problems like, "He's holding me back," or "She was not good for me." I remember reading a book in college about the psychology of management. I studied a theory that postulates that people have internal needs and are motivated by a desire to satisfy a set of needs. People are also wanting beings whose needs can influence their behavior. This theory makes it easy to understand how selfishness along with unrealistic expectations fit into our societal norms. Let's relate this theory to couples who are at different stages of growth and development. Let's look at two couples as examples.

Charles and Lynda attended the same college together and married shortly after their graduation. Lynda worked for two years as a registered nurse. Charles worked as a high-level executive in a large corporation. Lynda became pregnant unexpectedly with twins. They both decided Lynda would quit her job to care for the twins. Lynda's grandfather died and she inherited his estate, which was worth over $1 million. They were comfortable in their decision. Six months after Lynda quit her job, Charles decided to work part-time while he earned a law degree at a local university. Lynda was very supportive of Charles because she knew he was bright and could one day become a great lawyer. She used the money from her grandfather's estate to pay for his education.

After Charles graduated from law school five years later, he obtained a job at a prestigious law firm. Six months later, Lynda noticed he was not home often. Charles was spending more time in the company of his male and female colleagues attending parties and other functions. Soon, he lost interest in his wife because as he put it to her one day, "You are boring, and we don't have much in common anymore."

Charmaine, a doctor, earned more money than Steve, a self-employed entrepreneur. Charmaine divorced Steve because she felt he could not keep up with her social circle of friends and her personal interests that had changed from when they were first married. She felt Steve was too complacent and that he should strive for more.

These couples go through what many couples experience when priorities are misplaced. We must be aware of societal lies about what it takes to be fulfilled and happy. Our cultural norm is that whatever makes you happy is good. But the truth is, anyone who seeks happiness as a prime motivator in a relationship is setting himself or herself up for an enormous disappointment.

Happiness, bliss, and fantasy are fed to us by unrealistic television programs, romance novels, and even by couples who pretend to have it all together. Have you ever noticed that love stories usually have happy endings and that if there is a problem, the problem is resolved by simply finding someone else? This continues over and over until you finally find that person whom you feel meets your expectations. With the influence of media images, couples tend to compare their marriages to other marriages that they feel are far better. Unhealthy comparisons contribute to feelings of despair. Couples are cautioned to beware of unrealistic expectations and unhealthy comparisons.

Marriage involves a lifetime of adjusting to reality. Marriage doesn't kill an active imagination any more than it dampens our appreciation for members of the opposite sex. Marriage does, however, require us to redirect our passions exclusively and wholeheartedly toward our partners. We are called to sort out the godly from the evil, the lovely from the stained. We need to be aware of and alert to the influences and messages all around us that promote unhealthy fantasies.

The lust of the eyes subtly draws us away from the Word of God and eats away at our confidence in God. We see what the world has to offer and desire it above our relationship with God. We begin to place more credence in our own perspective of life than in God's commands and promises. Fueled by the lust for what we see, we grab for all we can get, believing that we need it, and deceived that God wants us to have it by wrongly assuming that God will withhold nothing good from us. We lustfully claim prosperity.

No temptation has overtaken you but such as is common to man; and God is faithful, who will not allow you to be tempted beyond what you are able, but will provide a way of escape also, that you may be able to endure it (1 Cor. 10:13).

. . . apprehend every thought as soon as it steps through the doorway of your mind.[6]

Focus your thoughts on the Word of God. Dispel those thoughts that your marriage seems terribly inadequate in comparison to others. Adam did not have anyone to compare Eve to. God made them perfectly suited for each other. He made you and your spouse perfectly suited for each other. Don't get caught up in comparisons. Comparison means we want what others have. This has become part of our culture of abundant things accompanied by the expectations that life should continually escalate to something better and easier.

Communicate to your mate your reasonable desires and discuss ways to liven things up. Discuss what each of you would like, whether this involves times spent alone, lovemaking, etc. Spend a great deal of time together alone. Communicate and pray together. Become physically and emotionally close to your spouse and let no one interfere with this closeness. Your fantasy should only be focused on your mate.

Does the Lord have unrealistic expectations of us? Or does He simply want us to look to Him to provide us with the desires of our hearts? As flawed women married to flawed men, couples will have the desires of their hearts if they work towards oneness in their marriage. Couples must work towards eliminating selfishness and focus more on developing a Christlike character. Couples should spend more time on learning what their individual godly roles are as husband, wife, and parent rather than spending energy on what is deficient in their mate. If couples do this, they will appreciate more the person God has given to them. Forget what the world says about how marriage should be.

"And do not be conformed to this world, but be transformed by the renewing of your mind, that you may prove what the will of God is, that which is acceptable and perfect" (Rom. 12:2).

The following are our personal testimonies of what can happen when worldly expectations in relationships are not met. These accounts were from before we accepted Jesus Christ as our personal savior and began studying the Word of God.

Sharon's Story

My idea of marriage was based on the fairy tale media images that man and woman meet, date, marry, have many children, and live happily ever after. I was captivated by fairy tales and love stories and romance novels. Yes, these dangerous and unhealthy media fantasies that feed into our perceptions and distort reality. *Leave It to Beaver, Ozzie and Harriet, Father Knows Best,* and *The Brady Bunch,* to name a few of many TV shows during the sixties and seventies, were four of my favorite TV shows. Television during that time was not as negative as it is today; however, these programs depicted families not like typical families that have real problems, but like families that always appeared to resolve their problems with little effort. No one ever raised their voice or appeared upset or angry and there was always a happy ending. In my late teens, like Sleeping Beauty, Cinderella, and so many other fairy tale figures, I began my search for prince charming.

At age nineteen, I thought that like magic my prince would marry me, we would have eight children, and we would live happily ever after. Compatibility was my criterion for finding my perfect mate. During the seventies, compatibility was based on the Zodiac signs. Well, I went through the process of elimination by excluding all those interested whose signs were not compatible with the sign "Cancer." Remember the days when you would meet a person and their first question to you was, "What's your sign?"

I grew up in a home with mom, dad, seven children, and two dogs. My parents had their share of ups and downs, but they always appeared to be able to work things out. They remained married for forty-three years until my father passed away. The sustenance of their forty-three-year marriage was because of their love for Jesus Christ and their strong commitment to family, each other, their children, and their grandchildren.

At age twenty I married my first husband. Reality set in very quickly. After the shock, I spent every day adjusting to unmet expectations. It was the same for him. We attended church sometimes out of habit because we were both raised in the church, but we had not truly accepted Jesus Christ as our personal savior. This marriage did not meet either of our expectations, and ten years later, we separated and then divorced shortly thereafter. A few years later I met my prince charming, who, I knew immediately would meet my expectations. We dated and fell in love. When he proposed, I was happy and immediately accepted his proposal. I remember thinking, "This marriage will definitely work because he is perfect for me and I love him, and I am a good woman and I would be good for him." We all moved in together. The reality and shock of this newly created blended family hit us very quickly.

Edward's Story

I, too, did not know what God's perfect plan is for marriage. I believed that since my expectations were not met in my first marriage, that I would truly find someone else who would treat me the way I felt I should be treated. I, too, always wanted to be married and live happily ever after. I divorced my first wife after many years of marriage.

My father died when I was eight years old; my mother raised five children and never remarried. I did not know or learn how marriage should be because there was no male role model or model marriage in our home and even if there had been, I still had my own belief of how marriage should be. I was married the first time at the tender young age of nineteen. Before my twentieth birthday my first daughter was born. My wife at that time and I were both still in college. God and church were nowhere in our lives. We struggled through the worldly ups and downs of a marriage until the girls were out of high school and in college and then we called it quits. After I met and courted Sharon, this wonderful princess who I knew would fulfill all my worldly expectations and would be my perfect mate, we were married. Reality set in immediately. It seemed that all at once this newly created blended family did not fulfill my high worldly expectations. When we dated, we did not spend time with her children. They visited their father every weekend. Since my children were grown and away at college at the time, I did not feel it was necessary for them to get to know Sharon. We decided that building a relationship with them was not necessary, since they were not moving into our home. When we all moved in together, it was like moving in with Sharon and three strangers. Because we did not have an agreement, nor did we think of establishing rules, the issues surfaced immediately. Sharon and I loved each other and tried very hard to struggle through the issues of children, former spouses, former in-laws, unmet expectations, and the many other issues unique to blended families.

We realized that we married different mates only to find a different set of issues. Our marriage has always been a good marriage; however, we were faced with the challenge of problems with the children that ultimately led to problems in our relationship. Only this time, we had no idea how to resolve these complex issues. We were led to church, joined church, and began studying the Word of God. We read self-help books concerning marriage, attended retreats and workshops on marriage, and we were still faced with unresolved issues unique to blended families.

We are very committed to each other and to the covenant of marriage. Divorce is not and never will be an option. We love each other very much and still enjoy each other immensely in spite of the problems we face. We know that without Jesus Christ in our lives we would not have made it this far.

Finally, we often hear the term the grass is greener on the other side. People constantly compare their mates to their ideal person hoping that one day this ideal person will come along. Well, with the exception of abusive situations, the grass is not greener on the other side. You leave one person and date or remarry someone else, only to get a different person with a different set of issues. We all come here with different genetic codes, innately selfish natures, and different issues. When you are seeking a mate, look for a person who has accepted Jesus Christ as his or her personal savior, who studies and attempts to live by the Word of God, or exemplifies the fruits of the spirit in his or her daily walk, who believes in a strong commitment of marriage and family and will love you unconditionally. Your ideal mate does not have to be perfect. None of us is perfect. We strongly suggest premarital Christian counseling.

We talk to married couples, singles, and also couples contemplating divorce. They struggle through issues, but in their minds, they feel there is someone else better. As they discuss what is lacking in their spouses they dwell on these issues. Different issues come with different people. It is true that every marriage has problems; however, exchanging the marriage you have for another relationship is almost always a losing move. Divorce can happen to anyone. But rather than fear divorce, couples should learn valuable lessons from the divorces of others and then use those lessons to strengthen their own marriages. Good marriages take work. You can't just coast along in the marriage without putting forth an effort to make it work, and you can't take each other for granted. You must work towards the goal of maturity in your marriage.

Through God's grace and forgiveness of our past sins, we were able to learn what God's perfect plan is for marriage. It has nothing to do with fairy tales, but rather with commitment, biblical agape love, mutual respect, and mutual submission to each other and to God.

How We Handle Problems

To gain a better understanding of how we handle problems the way we do, let's go to the Garden of Eden. When things don't work out with your spouse according to the worldly concept of marriage, partners have a tendency to do exactly what Adam did in the Garden of Eden. That is, he shifted the blame to Eve. This is what happened: The Lord made the tree of life and the tree of the knowledge of good and evil. And the Lord God gave man orders saying, "You may freely take of the fruit of every tree of the garden. But of the fruit of the tree of the knowledge of good and evil, you may not take, for on the day when you take of it, death will certainly come to you." The serpent Satan was wiser than any beast of the field, and he said to the woman, "Has God truly said you may not take fruit of any tree in the garden?" Eve replied, "We may take of the fruit of the trees in the garden except of the fruit of the tree in the middle of the garden. If we take of it, death will come." The serpent said, "Death will not come to you, For that on the day when you take of its fruit, your eyes will be open and you will be as God having the knowledge of good and evil." So Eve took the fruit and also gave it to her husband. Their eyes opened, and they were conscious they had no clothing. They made coats of leaves and they hid from the Lord. The Lord said, "Where are you?" Adam replied, "I was full of fear because I was without clothing." And the Lord said, "Who gave you the knowledge you were without clothing? Have you taken of the fruit of the tree, which I said you were not to take?" And Adam said, "The woman who you gave me, she gave me the fruit of the tree, and I took it." Adam shifted the blame to the Lord for giving him Eve and then to Eve who took the fruit from the forbidden tree (Gen. 2, 3).

Isn't this familiar when we are arguing with our spouse? Aren't we quick to shift the blame to someone else and not take responsibility for our part in the problem? Conflict between husband and wife started in the Garden of Eden. Satan does not intend for marriages to work as evidenced in the Garden of Eden.

When John and Kathy attended their first counseling session, their counselor pointed out to them the problem of sin and used the first marriage as an example. John and Kathy were informed by their Christian counselor that God hates divorce. The counselor stated, "Marriage is a divine institution the Lord uses to teach His children about their relationship to Him. God made man and woman as one flesh." The counselor felt that they have a workable situation if they could get beyond the blame. The counselor stated:

> Think of this analogy: Adam could not divorce Eve and take another because there was no other to take. A rib was taken out of Adam to make Eve. If his other rib was taken away from him, wouldn't this make Adam incomplete? How could he take a whole (one flesh) and split it in half? In other words, how can you unmake something that was intended to be one flesh? If you try to tear it apart, it becomes a mess.

> With the fall of humankind, the divine purpose and function of marriage were damaged by sin and the marriage relationship often destroyed. The relational aspect of God's image, reflected in marriage, became marred because of sin. Sin brought polygamy, concubinage, incest, adultery, rape, prostitution and all kinds of immorality that have damaged or destroyed the marriage relationship (Lev. 18, 20; Rom. 1:26–32). Married covenants have been violated (Mal. 2:14). Because of sin, divorce became prevalent and Moses sought to regulate it using a Certificate of Divorce (Deut. 24:1–4; Matt. 19:8). Divorce is not instituted or ordained by God; rather it is generated by sin and is contrary to God's ideal for marriage. (Mal. 2:14)[7]

The counselor informed John and Kathy of the consequences of divorce and remarriage. People attempt to change God's word to make divorce applicable to their situation. There are consequences of divorce. Matt. 19:9 states, "And I say to you, whoever divorces his wife, except for sexual immorality, and marries another, commits adultery; and whoever marries her who is divorced commits adultery."

> Divorce is permitted in certain situations (Mal. 2:14) when one has committed adultery/fornication. Adultery severs the marriage relationship in the New Testament. This is not required and should be the last alternative. In Matt. 5:27–32 Jesus states that lust as well as divorce are the moral equivalents of adultery. Divorce produces adultery in the remarriage (Mark 10:11–12) except in the case of fornication (Matt. 5:31–32). Corinthians 7:1–16 argues married people should stay married. Spouses should not leave a spouse. If a spouse leaves/divorces, there are only two options: (1) remain unmarried, (2) reconcile. Remarriage is not an option. Believers

should not divorce an unbelieving spouse (v. 12–13). If the unbeliever leaves, the believing partner is not bound to the principle about maintaining the marriage. The marriage is dissolved; however, Paul does not address the issue of remarriage.

Believers must love and accept divorced people and seek to encourage them in reconciliation and godly ways.

John asked, "Well what about those who have divorced and remarried?" The counselor replied:

They must know that divorce is never God's choice. However, whenever divorce occurs for whatever reason, God works redemptively when the person who has experienced this tragedy has repented and desires reconciliation to God. Matt. 19:8 states, He said to them, "Moses, because of the hardness of your hearts, permitted you to divorce your wives, but from the beginning it was not so." When remarriage follows divorce, there is no turning back. God sees this relationship as permanent and binding, and this holy covenant cannot be broken. He observes that the sinful world makes this tragedy a reality. Therefore, if any man be in Christ, he is a new creature, old things are passed away, behold, all things are become new (2 Cor. 5:17). Jesus Christ gives no divine directive nor even acceptable excuses for breaking this holy covenant but rather observes that because of the hardness of the human heart it makes this tragedy a reality in this sinful world (Matt. 19:8). With, God's forgiveness, it is as if it never happened. No sin or tragedy is beyond God's forgiveness. The remarried couple must seek anew an understanding of God's plan for marriage and commit wholeheartedly to pursuing his plan and consider their vows of marriage

before the Lord.[9] Does this answer your question?

"Yes," replied John.

John and Kathy understood the reasons divorce must not be an option and that God hates divorce because it is contrary to His original plan. They also understood that Jesus upheld the idea of permanent marriage, making it clear that divorce is equivalent to adultery because it breaks the oneness of marriage. They prayed that the Lord reveal to them what they must do to promote peace and harmony in their family.

The tearing apart of a marriage is very painful and leaves lasting scars. Jesus gives no divine directive, nor even acceptable excuses, for breaking this holy covenant.

The role of the church and of believers in regard to remarriages must always be redemptive. With God's grace, no sin or tragedy is beyond God's forgiveness. With God's forgiveness, it is as if it never happened. Remarried people must understand God's perfect plan for marriage and commit to building their home on a solid foundation. These couples should minister to encourage others who are married to not break God's marriage covenant.

Unclean Thoughts

"Now, we are on our way to oneness," John said. "Some people may say that they understand the sanctity of marriage and that divorce is not an option. But what about the current problems we are experiencing in our relationship with each other?"

The counselor stated that Satan will put a negative thought or thoughts in couples' minds about their spouses and cause them to focus on reasons to divorce instead of reasons to stay together. Always replace these negative

Negative Worldly Attitudes

1. Love is better the second time around.
2. I married my mate for the wrong reasons.
3. We were too young and we grew apart.
4. I am unhappy and miserable.
5. My spouse is financially irresponsible and never makes good decisions.
6. My spouse cheated on me. I don't want to leave, but I can't seem to forgive.
7. I thought we were compatible.
8. My spouse is not affectionate.
9. We don't love each other anymore.
10. My spouse competes with me.
11. We don't trust each other anymore.
12. We are not attracted to each other anymore.
13. I'd rather live alone, and I don't want to be married anymore.
14. We don't have time for each other.
15. My spouse can't conceive.
16. Our sex has reduced from every day to once every two months.

thoughts with Scriptures. Remember, the Word of God has an answer for every problem.

We are providing an example of how couples can address problems and dispel negative thinking and unclean thoughts. When conflict arises, couples tend to blame each other, overreact, withdraw, and not forgive. Bitterness builds to isolation. Isolation leads to divorce. We attempt to use our own minds to resolve issues instead of seeking the Lord. Worldly wisdom puts us out of God's will. We attempt to change our spouses to meet our expectations and are discouraged because we feel our mate is not living up to how we feel he or she should be. If you are unable to resolve issues in

your marriage by studying on your own, seek Christian counseling.

In some situations, one spouse may not be saved. Pray for your spouse and seek resources that will help you lead your spouse to the Lord.

Abusive behavior, whether physical, mental, or emotional, must not be tolerated. Violence or physical abuse in intimate relationships and towards children is very common. Harmful behavior also includes verbal outbursts of yelling and insults that may eventually lead to violence. What leads to such harmful behavior between people who supposedly love each other? Psychologists have suggested many contributing factors such as social pressures that create stress, cultural values that condone violence, personality pathologies, and drug and alcohol addiction.[10]

Verbal abuse can be as harmful as physical abuse. Verbal abuse leads to impairment of self-esteem. "A man will be satisfied with good by the fruit of his mouth, and the recompense of a man's hands will be rendered to him" (Prov. 12:14). This also applies to women. Words are very powerful, and if not used appropriately will lead to the destruction of a relationship.

"Death and life are in the power of the tongue, and those who love it will eat its fruit" (Prov. 18:21). Couples often say very hurtful things to each other.

"Let no corrupt communication proceed out of your mouth, but what is good for necessary edification, that it may impart grace to the hearers" (Eph. 4:29).

Do not use harmful words but only helpful words, the kind that build up and provide what is needed, so that what you say will do good to those who hear you.

"The words of a wise man's mouth are gracious, but the lips of a fool shall swallow him up" (Eccles. 10:12).

Replace Worldly Attitudes with Biblical Scriptures

1. Many waters cannot quench love . . . (Song Of Songs 8:7)
2. What God has joined together, let no man put asunder (Matt. 19:6).
3. "This is now bone of my bones, and flesh of my flesh . . ." (Gen. 2:23)." . . . and they shall become one flesh" (Gen. 2:24).
4. "Know that the Lord He is God: It is He who made us and not we ourselves. We are His people and the sheep of His Pasture" (Ps. 100:3).
5. "Therefore, to him who knows to do good and does not do it, to him it is sin" (James 4:17).
6. Jesus condemned adultery (Mark 10:11–12). Adulterers can receive God's forgiveness (John 8:3–11); Love for an adulterous spouse (Hos. 3:1); If you forgive, God will forgive you (Matt. 6:14–15).
7. "It is not good for man to be alone; I will make him a help mate for him" (Gen. 2:18).
8. "Wives submit to your husbands . . . Husbands love your wives . . . " (Col. 3: 18–19).
9. God's love is better than life (Ps. 63:3); We are commanded to love one another (John 3:11); We are commanded to do the acts of love (1 John 3:17).
10. Roles of husband and wife (Eph. 5:21–33).
11. Cast all your cares upon the Lord (1 Pet. 5:7).
12. ". . . and rejoice with the wife of your youth . . . " (Prov. 5:18–21).
13. "Two are better than one, Because they have a good reward for their labor. For if they fall, one will lift up his companion. But woe to him who is alone when he falls, he has no one to help him up . . . " (Eccles. 4:9–12).
14. "Live joyfully with the wife whom you love all the days of your vain life which he has given you . . . " (Eccles. 9:9).
15. Beloved, but barren (1 Sam. 1:2–7); God's timing (Gen. 20:17).
16. "Let the husband render to his wife the affection due her and also the wife to her husband. The wife does not have authority over her body, but the husband does. And likewise, the husband does not have authority over his own body, but the wife does" (1 Cor. 7:3–4).

Caution to couples concerning sex-related issues: Immediately address negative emotions or physical intimacy will be affected.

Mental and emotional abuse can be as harmful as physical abuse. A major source of stress and depression is low self-esteem and lack of self-confidence that comes from being constantly put down by those closest to us. As the wife of one well-known doctor puts it, "I never do anything right according to my husband." They have been married for thirty years. There is nothing she can do to please him.

Church leaders long to see a person freed from the terror of an abusive spouse, yet they are uncomfortable advising action that has no clear biblical grounds for divorce and remarriage. A person who is being physically abused should never take the blame for the abuse, but should take immediate steps to ensure safety by involving the authorities and seeking shelter.

If you have been abused, God is your comforter and offers love and acceptance. Reach out to the Lord, turn to the Church, family, and authorities for protection. Put your hope in the Lord, for He is our protector.

Read and meditate on Psalm 31. In You, O Lord, I put my trust; Let me never be ashamed; Deliver me in Your righteousness. Bow down Your ear to me, Deliver me speedily; Be my rock of refuge, A fortress of defense to save me. For you are my rock and my fortress; Therefore, for Your name's sake, Lead me and guide me. Pull me out of the net which they have secretly laid for me, For You are my strength

There are examples in the Bible of how conflict was handled by couples: 1 Sam. 25 describes a man named Nabal and his wife, Abigail. Nabal was wealthy and a hard man to live with. He was surly, mean, harsh, and overbearing. He was impossible to reason with. This marriage was an arranged marriage. Abigail handled Nabal by making the best of a bad situation.

David's men set out to destroy Nabal and his household. Abigail felt she should act quickly to limit the damage her husband had done. She took two hundred loaves of bread, two skins of wine, five dressed sheep, roasted grain, raisins, and cakes of pressed figs and loaded them on donkeys. She did not tell Nabal she was doing this. She rode with her servants towards David and his men. When she saw David she bowed down before him with her face to the ground. David said to Abigail, "Praise be to the Lord, the God of Israel, who has sent you today to meet me. May you be blessed for your good judgment and for keeping me from bloodshed this day and from avenging myself with my own hands" (32–33). David saw Abigail's independent action, contrary to Nabal's wishes, as being from God. Abigail was a wise woman who acted in the best interests of her household and of her husband. In going against Nabal's wishes, she saved his life. This woman is submissive, but wise also in trying to limit the damage caused by her husband in her home.

For further reading, read the story of Jacob, Rachel, and Leah (Gen. 29–31). Leah lived with a man who did not love her. She was the unfavored wife of Jacob. Out of Leah's sadness came a rich blessing for Israel. When the Lord saw that Leah was not loved, he opened her womb, but Rachel was barren. God was not blind to Leah's plight. He saw the ache in her heart and did something about her situation. The sovereign God saw Leah's need and moved to meet it. It was Leah who gave birth to Judah, from whom came Israel's greatest king, David, and from whom came our Lord Jesus Christ.

Leah, the sister of Rachel, lived in a very difficult situation and survived. Like her, we too are fallen people in a fallen world. We are people scarred by alienation from each other and from ourselves. Life seldom, if ever, comes to us in a way that is fully satisfying. Most of the time it comes with an edge of dissatisfaction—not quite enough love or care, not quite enough honor or esteem. Like Leah we can focus on what we lack and be miserable. Or, also like Leah, we can decide to focus on what we have and make up our minds that this time we will praise the Lord. How do you live with a husband or wife who doesn't love you? You change your focus. In the process, you will not only end up exclaiming, as did Leah, how happy you are but you will someday find that God has worked his miracle through your sadness touching the world with blessing through you.

24

Chapter 5

Commitment to Changing Self and Building Character

But the fruit of the Spirit is love, joy, peace, longsuffering, kindness, good-
ness, faithfulness, gentleness, self-control. Against such there is no law.
And those who are Christ's have crucified the flesh with its passions and
desires. If we live in the Spirit, let us also walk in the Spirit.
—Galatians 5:22–25

Couples must be committed to surrendering to God, growing spiritually, and praying that they grow to have a Christlike character. Developing character is important to promoting a harmonious and peaceful home. Character building equips us with the necessary tools to face adversity and to teach our children godly morals and values. It also strengthens our Christian walk.

The fruit of the Holy Spirit is the result of the Holy Spirit's presence in the lives of believers (Gal. 5:22–23). It is the evidence of a spirit-filled sancti-fied life through faith. It is the result of Christ living in you (Gal. 2:20, 5:16–21). Producing good fruit requires effort on the Christian's part and a cooperation with the Holy Spirit.

The fruit of the spirit can be described as: an active love for God and one's fellow man; a rejoicing in all kinds of circumstances; peaceful-ness and serenity of character and peacemaking among people; patience and longsuffering with persons, some of whom may not be easy to get along with; kindness toward others, goodness that seeks to aid others; faithfulness and dependability in one's relationship with God and other people; gentle-ness and meekness in accepting God's will and in dealing with others; and the ability to keep oneself in check and under control in all kinds of circumstances.[1]

As we grow in our relationship with the Lord, we develop unselfish love, joy, peace, and faithfulness. As we develop and build relationships with others, we are challenged to reflect His forgiveness, patience, kindness, good-ness, gentleness, and self-control.

Couples must accept all members within the family. "Accept one another, then, just as Christ accepts you, in order to bring praise to God" (Rom. 15:7). Acceptance is something that everyone needs, but does not always get. "So we make it our goal to please him, whether we are at home in the body or away from it" (2 Cor. 5:9).

25

Christ accepts us. How would we feel if he applied conditions to his acceptance of believers and also to those who are alien to him? "I will call them my people who are not my people; and I will call her my loved one who is not my loved one" (Rom. 9:25).

Whatever your circumstances are at the time, you must accept it as part of God's plan for your life. Don't argue with the Creator.

"Woe to him who quarrels with his Maker, to him who is but a potsherd among the potsherds on the ground. Does the clay say to the potter, what are you making? Does your work say, He has no hands?" (Isa. 45:9).

We must always forgive. Jesus wants us to have a forgiving spirit. "If you come across your enemy's ox or donkey wandering off, be sure to take it back to him. If you see the donkey of someone who hates you fallen down under its load, do not leave it there; be sure you help him with it" (Exod. 23:4–5).

Why does God want us to forgive others and forgive ourselves? "I, even I, am He who blots out your transgressions, for my own sake, and remembers your sins no more" (Isa. 43:25). Pray for those who refuse to forgive you for past sins.

Forgiveness is a power tool in marriage that if used frequently and immediately can make a marriage go from a good marriage to an excellent marriage. Ask your children to forgive you if you unknowingly accused them of doing something wrong that you later find out they did not do. Verbally communicate, "I'm sorry. I will try to never hurt you again. Will you forgive me?"

We must be kind towards one another. Kindness was shown by Ruth towards her mother-in-law, Naomi (Ruth 1). Kindness was shown by Joseph towards Mary, Jesus' mother.

She was pledged to be married to Joseph, but before they came together, she was found to be with child through the Holy Spirit (Matt. 1:18). "Because Joseph her husband was a righteous man and did not want to expose her to public disgrace, he had in mind to divorce her quietly" (Matt. 1:19). But after he had considered this, an angel of the Lord appeared to him in a dream and said, "Joseph son of David, do not be afraid to take Mary as your wife, because that which is conceived in her is from the Holy Spirit. She will give birth to a son, and you are to give him the name Jesus, because he will save people from their sins (Matt. 1:20–21)."[2]

Be kind to one another always. In times of hurt, the natural tendency is to hurt others because we are hurting. Jacob's son Joseph wept when his brothers threw themselves down before him and asked Joseph for forgiveness for treating him badly. Joseph responded by telling them to not be afraid. He reassured them and spoke kindly to them (Gen. 50:15–21).

Showing patience is a very important attribute to exhibit in any relationship. God is very patient with us and does not turn His back on us. Frustration surfaces when people are confronted with challenging issues or when a person's selfish nature appears and the person is unable to have his or her way. Feelings of discouragement, bafflement, and sometimes anger surface when a desire cannot be fulfilled. "In your anger do not sin; when you are on your beds, search your hearts and be silent" (Ps. 4:4).

Patience is having the "capacity of calm endurance, tolerance of someone over a period of time without complaint, though not necessarily without annoyance. An admirable endurance of a trying situation usually through passiveness which comes out of understanding."[3]

Gentleness or meekness is a considerate or kind disposition. A gentle person is amicable and patient, not harsh or violent. People should be gentle toward one another. In families, husbands should be gentle towards their wives and wives toward their husbands and parents towards their children. Jesus was gentle towards little children.

People were bringing babes to Jesus to have him touch them. When the disciples saw this, they rebuked them. But Jesus called the children to him and said, Let the children come to me, and do not hinder them, for the kingdom of God belongs to such as these. I tell you the truth, anyone who will not receive the kingdom of God like a little child will never enter it (Luke 18:15–17).

Longsuffering encompasses patience, endurance, forgiveness, steadfastness, and forbearance. It is patiently enduring wrongs or difficulties. Believers who walk in the Spirit develop a longsuffering attitude that no circumstances can destroy.

Faithfulness, is the quality descriptive of God's ongoing relationship to the world and a believer's desired relationship to God and to other. Steadfast loyalty and unwavering trust are considered essential virtues for personal and spiritual growth. Faithfulness is a manifestation of the fruits of the Spirit that pertains to loyalty and trustworthiness. Believers are called to faithfulness to God, to self, and to others. A believer is challenged to maintain steadfast trust in God even amidst trials and suffering.[4]

"Be faithful until death, and I will give you the crown of life" (Rev. 2:10).

The reward of walking in faith is the experience of Joy. Joy comes as a result of faith and obedience (John 15:10, 11). Sin can rob a person of joy. True joy is evident regardless of circumstances. Biblical joy is clearly different from earthly, temporal pleasures that are bound to circumstances. True joy enables you to enjoy all that God has given; family, health, friends, opportunities, and salvation.[5]

Peace is also the result of having the right relationship with God and with others. Inner, spiritual peace is experienced by any believer who walks in the Spirit despite surroundings. The God of peace, who offers salvation, also promised His presence and power in the lives of his children. His presence creates in us a quiet confidence regardless of circumstances, people or things.[6]

When peace is present there is no room for worry.

Self-discipline or self-control is essential to personal development and spiritual growth. Christians must learn to discipline outward behaviors and inward feelings in order to be godly. Words and actions as well as thoughts and passions must be acceptable to God (Ps. 19:14). A disciplined life involves genuine personal commitment to obey God's statutes and frequently it requires lifestyle changes. Scripture teaches that self control is the crowning fruit of the Holy Spirit (Gal. 5:22). Without self-control, the believer has little opportunity to experience fully the blessings of God.[7]

The character trait love is an unconditional devotion to others. Biblical love demands going beyond merely a particular behavior to include a certain inner attitude that is a positive inner response. This does not mean a person must accept sinful behavior. Instead he or she should

27

attempt to restore the sinner to the right relationship with God. Agape love is Christlike love or selfless love. Unselfish, loyal, benevolent concern for the well-being of others is the greatest gift of all. Biblical love is not envious, proud, self-centered, rude, or provoking. Without love the gifts of the Spirit are deemed worthless and the fruit of the spirit is incomplete. Christian love is eternal. Love never fails. It is a permanent, unconditional concern for others that results from the indwelling power of the Holy Spirit, rather than from human effort or desire.[8]

Throughout this book, we have discussed the issue of the development of love between the stepparent and stepchild. We indicate that there is no instant love and that love has to develop over time as the relationship grows. The unconditional commitment and devotion stepparents and stepchildren show towards each other is love, even though the words may not be spoken. A stepparent may not feel love towards a stepchild or a stepchild may not feel love towards a stepparent, but according to the definition of biblical love, love is not a feeling but rather a condition of commitment.

Having a generous heart is important. All that we have belongs to Christ. Our homes, cars, money, children, all of our worldly possessions. If we truly believe that all our possessions belong to God then we should not have a problem giving. A generous heart is evidence that the Holy Spirit is working in your life. When you truly have a giving heart, that is, without conditions, you will experience God's blessings and rewards.

What produces a strong character? Self-confidence which comes from being at peace with God and knowing who you are in Christ. A strong character is

How To Love:

The following examples show how love can be applied in a family relationship:

Is Patient—forgives his sloppiness and waits until he picks his socks up off the floor. Forgives the children when they make the same mistake over again.

Is Kind—rubs her back, legs, and feet when she has to run behind a toddler every day.

Does Not Envy—because husband makes more money than wife.

Is Not Boastful—Does not communicate to another the successes of her child when that person's child is not doing well.

Is Not Proud—admits that he was incorrect.

Is Not Rude—speaks to each family member as well as others respectfully in private and in public. Speaks appropriately without being loud, boisterous, or putting others down.

Is Not Self-seeking—gives up what he wants for the needs of others.

Is Not Easily Angered—does not react in a rage or raise voice to family or others.

Keeps No Record of Wrongs—forgives always.

Does Not Delight in Evil—takes no part in evil wrongdoing.

Rejoices in the Truth—faces real issues.

Always Protects—protects both wife and family.

Always Trusts—avoids suspicious attitude towards family members and others.

Always Hopes—looks to the future.

Always Perseveres—keeps on the whole armor of God in the face of adversity.

also produced by having the right priorities, following the right example, obedience to God's commands, a steady diet of God's Word, relying on the

28

Blameless—God expects men to be above reproach. This all-inclusive term summarizes all the qualities described in 1 Tim. 3. It means that a man must have a pattern of life that is consistent with biblical standards.

Husband of one wife—A married man must be faithful to his wife. He keeps his marriage vows and does not toy with any type of sexual immorality. Literally "a one-woman man," this qualification has a broader possible meaning that a man is not to be a "womanizer" or a flirt. His heart is not to be afire with lust (Matt. 5:27, 28)

Temperate—Gene Getz has stated that "a man who is temperate does not lose his physical, psychological, and spiritual orientation. He remains stable and steadfast, and his thinking is clear." Such a man is balanced in his living, not given to destructive extremes.

Soberminded—This term is closely related to the term temperate. It refers to the quality of being sensible in thinking and actions, exhibiting sound judgment.

Of good behavior—A man should be respectable and honorable in his actions.

Hospitable—The Greek term behind the word literally means "loving strangers." In a general sense, this term refers to friendliness and a willingness to help those in needs.

Able to teach—This characteristic carries two possible meanings. It may mean that a man should have the ability to instruct others about the Christian faith. Or it could mean that a man is to be "teachable." If we combine these two elements, the term refers to an ability to teach others without arrogance.

Not given to wine—A man of God is not one who is controlled by alcohol (Eph. 5:18). In our day and age, this could be applied to illegal drugs as well. God does not want us to abuse our bodies or cloud our minds.

Not violent—The Greek word literally means "not striker." Temper tantrums do not please God. This includes both violent actions and words.

Gentle—A God-honoring man, according to this term, would be gracious, kind, forbearing, and considerate of others.

Not quarrelsome—A man is not to be one who is always looking for an argument or stirring up trouble.

Not greedy for money nor covetous—Acquiring money and possessions should not be a priority. Jesus and Paul warned against a preoccupation with money (Matt. 6:19–21; 1 Tim. 6:10).

Rules his own house well—The man is the head of the home. He is responsible to see that his relationships with his wife and children are good. He is to be a good manager of home life.

Having his children under submission—A father is to be a respected leader at home, a man who does all that is in his power to train and discipline his children.

Not a novice—A new believer who becomes a leader before he is mature in his faith and practice runs a risk of falling into pride. This is warning that a man is not to take on responsibilities that he is not mature enough to handle. Men must guard themselves against pride.

Good testimony among those outside—A man must develop a good reputation with non-Christians. He is to have a consistent faith that will be a strong witness to unbelievers.

Willingness to serve, humility—A man must have the ability to live in harmony with others, be willing to associate with people of low position, and not be conceited (John 13:1–7; Rom. 12:15).

Sexual purity—Sex was designed for the marriage bed (Rom. 13:13–14; Heb. 13:4).

Commitment to Church—God did not intend the Christian life to be a game of solitaire. He designed the church to meet our needs and for us to serve others. You should agree on this issue with your future mate (Eph. 4:1–16; Heb. 10:24–25).[9]

strength of the Spirit, making right choices—living out the Christian faith, doing what is right no matter what, trusting and depending on God, and learning from others.

Read the Sermon on the Mount in Matt. 5. Our pastor taught a series of lessons at our church on the Beatitudes. The overall message was that if we are going to truly change our behavior, we must change our attitudes because attitudes determine behavior. The *Women's Study Bible* Commentary states that Jesus identified wrong attitudes as triggering other sins. This Bible lists Beatitudes for Women; however, these attitudes can be applied to men also: Humility (Luke 4:16–21); Sensitivity (Luke 19:41); Meekness (Matt. 6:33); Obedience (Luke 1:53); Compassion (Luke 1:58); Holiness (Ps. 24:4–6); Reconciliation (Rom. 3:25, 12:18); Commitment (Luke 13:35); and Patience (1 Pet. 2:19).

In conclusion, it is important to know what the fruits of the Spirit and Beatitudes are in order to make them a part of your Christian life. The believer will eventually become more Christlike in character and actions. God promises to use all of our life experiences including any evil that has been done against us for our good. Adversity changes our character as we become more like the Lord. Respond biblically. All things are for our good if we love God. Helen Keller said:

Character cannot be developed in ease and quiet. Only through experience of trial and suffering can the soul be strengthened.

Chapter 6

What Is God's Perfect Plan For Marriage?

Therefore, a man shall leave his father and mother and be joined to his wife, and they shall become one flesh. —Genesis 2:24

Since marriage is a condition of life that nine out of ten people enter, it is important to know what God's perfect plan is for marriage. This knowledge will help strengthen your marriage and it will help you combat the enemy's attack on your marriage. Satan's ploy is to rob and steal from marriages as evidenced in the Garden of Eden.

The marriage relationship and home must be built on a solid foundation. That is, Christ must be the center of your life or it will fall apart. Jesus Christ taught many of His lessons by using parables. The parable of a man who built his house on a solid foundation is found in the conclusion of Jesus Christ's Sermon on the Mount.

Therefore, whoever hears these sayings of Mine, and does them, I will liken him to a wise man who built his house on a rock: And the rain descended, the floods came, and the winds blew and beat on that house; and it did not fall, for it was founded on the rock. Now everyone who hears these sayings of Mine, and does not do them, will be like a foolish man who built his house on the sand: and the rain descended, the floods came, and the winds blew, and beat on that house; and it fell. And great was its fall (Matt. 7:24–27).

Is your house built on a solid foundation? Is it able to weather the storms? For your home to be built on a solid foundation, it must contain believers who have a strong faith and trust in God. "Through wisdom a house is built, and by understanding it is established; by knowledge the rooms are filled with all precious and pleasant riches" (Prov. 24:3, 4).

Marriage continues to be the most enduring evidence of a couple's love and commitment and is celebrated in every culture of the world by ceremonies and rituals with a hoped-for outcome of love that will deepen over the years. This marriage is cemented by events such as bearing and raising children, weathering economic and emotional ups and downs, surviving serious illnesses or other setbacks, and sharing a social life and financial commitments. Godly marriages were designed for the companionship and happiness of man, to increase the population by raising godly seeds, and to prevent fornication.

The solid foundation principle implies that when married couples stop looking to each other to have needs fulfilled and instead look to God, harmony and oneness is achieved.

Worldly View of Marriage

The worldly view of what constitutes a happy marriage is a distorted view. We enter into this relationship with little or no training. We are influenced by this view as we begin our search for the ideal mate. Consequently, we embrace and select a mate based on the worldly criteria of what we should look for in a mate. There are endless and inconsistent articles in magazines and books on what to look for in a mate. There are numerous articles written about what attracts men to women and women to men. Radio or television dating programs make it appear difficult for people to make that "love connection." We select the ideal person based on our worldly criteria and then can't understand why we are disillusioned when the person displays a character flaw that we did not know existed. We not only look at physical characteristics, which are usually the initial attraction to a person, but we also have a long list of other qualities we are looking for that are not the godly qualities we should look for. Some people search for that perfect person when the person looking is not flawless.

In chapter 4 we discussed how these unrealistic expectations are based on the worldly view and how these expectations can be carried into the marriage. Couples expect marriage to fulfill their need for affection, sexual intimacy, companionship, family, conversation, financial security, and social acceptance. Many enter marriage expecting the marriage to solve their current personal problems or the problems that may be an extension of unresolved childhood issues. Many enter marriage with a predetermined idea of what they want their partner to become with the goal of changing the person to become the ideal mate. Some enter marriage with the understanding that each partner will have a great deal of freedom, more than most couples are comfortable with, and the expectation that few demands will be placed on them.

God intended for marriage to be a lifetime commitment; however, this is not the situation today. Long marriages are disintegrating and the divorce rate is soaring. Based on a 1996 Vital Statistics report at the Center for Health Statistics, "there are 2,344,000 marriages and 1,150,000 divorces in the U.S. annually. The likelihood of new marriages ending in divorce is 43% based on 1988 data."[1] People change, situations differ, and dreams are shattered. But the same God who made marriage made it to endure the disappointments and predictable seasons of life that mark all good relationships. God can help you overcome the cycles of expectation, personal problems, and disillusionment and he will lead you towards fulfillment, contentment, and peace you never thought could exist in your relationship and life.

The Marriage Covenant

After we meet this wonderful, flawless person and fall in love, we decide to marry. At the wedding, there are beautiful flowers everywhere. The bride and groom are very happy as they exchange their vows with emphasis, undying love, and tears falling down their glowing faces. The vows are repeated, "I do take you to be my wedded husband, my wedded wife, to have and to hold from this day forward, for better, for worse, for richer, for poorer, in sickness and in health, to love, to honor, to cherish and to protect, forsaking all others as long as we both shall live." When couples exchange vows, they are committing themselves to each other in the presence of God and they are making a promise to God that they vow to care for and love each other until death separates them. These vows are the couple's marriage covenant to each other—not a business deal or contract, but a covenant. A covenant is an agreement between two parties and must not be broken. Marriage is a covenant relationship that forms the basis of our marriage, family, and church relationships (Mal. 2:4).

The marriage covenant was established by God in the Garden of Eden between Adam and Eve. The marriage was to be perfect in its establishment. God was aware of Adam's need for companionship. The couple must leave and cleave and be joined together as one. Cleave means to have a strong bond by unconditional love, and an acceptance stronger than they would have if they were separate. Leave is to be free from the influence of others outside of the marriage bond between husband and wife. Man and woman are to lay aside all that pertains to their old loyalties and lifestyle of separate goals and plans and join to one another. Thus, the couple must leave parents and physically, emotionally, and financially transfer dependence from parents to their mate. No other human relationship is to supersede the bond between husband and wife. This does not mean they are to ignore their parents and not care for them.

God never intended for man to be alone.

It is not good that a man should be alone; I will make him a helper comparable to him (Gen. 2:18).

Therefore a man shall leave his father and mother and be joined to his wife, and they shall become one flesh (Gen. 2:24).

The Broken Covenant

As a result of sin, man and woman rejected the Creator's plan for marriage and decided to do things their own way. The roles of man and woman as a result of sin became conflicting and in disharmony. God cursed man and women for the sin in the Garden of Eden. Pain resulted for the woman in giving birth and she would resist her husband's leadership role just as his rule over her would be distorted. The ground was cursed for Adam's sake. Adam was to eat of it all the days of his life.

Thorns and thistles it shall bring forth for Adam, and he shall eat the herb of the field. In the sweat of Adams face, he shall eat bread until he returns to the ground, for out of it he was taken; for dust he was and to dust he will return (Gen. 3:18–19).

Adam and Eve experienced spiritual warfare until the end of their time.

Unequally Yoked

Couples who have accepted Jesus Christ as their personal savior must pray that their marriage be strengthened. I heard a minister on television discussing relationships, marriage, and the reason why couples should not be unequally yoked. He made the statement, "Why date and/or consider marrying someone that is not saved? This is like going to a graveyard to talk to the dead." If you are already married to an unsaved person, pray for the salvation of your spouse. Do not preach to the unsaved person—pray instead. Prayer binds Satan. A quiet and gentle spirit is effective in leading a spouse to Christ. Concentrate on being the best spouse you can be by exhibiting a godly character at all times. Your light will shine and eventually you will lead your spouse to the Lord by the example you have set. Pray that your spouse becomes a child of God and dies to self. Pray that the Holy Spirit will dwell in you and your partner. After your spouse accepts the Lord Jesus Christ as his or her personal savior, you both must work towards not violating spiritual principles, which causes couples to work against each other and against God. This violation causes separation from each other and from God. You cannot seek to change God's plan according to your desires. There can be no unity, contentment, peace, or harmony, only a house divided.

Responsibilities of Marriage

Marriage is a threefold miracle. It is a biological miracle by which two become one flesh; it is a social miracle through which two families are grafted together; it is a spiritual miracle in that the marriage relationship imitates the union of Christ and his bride the church (Eph. 5:23–27).

Our Father's original plan for marriage is one in which the wife is to be an equal partner to be loved and protected. Paul gave instructions to husbands and wives concerning their individual roles and responsibilities.

Both husband and wife must submit to one another in fear of God.

Wives, submit to your own husbands, as to the Lord. For the husband is head of the wife, as also Christ is head of the church; and He is the Savior of the body. Therefore, just as the church is subject to Christ, so let the wives be to their own husbands in everything.

Husbands love your wives, just as Christ also loved the church and gave Himself for her, that He might sanctify and cleanse her with the washing of water by the word, that He might present her to Himself a glorious church, not having spot or wrinkle or any such thing, but that she should be holy and without blemish. So husbands ought to love their own wives as their own bodies; he who loves Himself. For no one ever hated his own flesh, but nourishes and cherishes it, just as the Lord does the church. For we are members of His body, of His flesh and of His bones. For this reason a man shall leave his father and mother and be joined to his wife, and the two shall become one flesh (Eph. 5:22–31).

When both husband and wife know the Lord as their personal Savior, the Holy Spirit lives in their hearts. As they submit to the Lord they are enabled to follow His directions. The husband will be empowered to love his wife as Christ loved the church and the wife will be inspired to submit as unto the Lord. The atmosphere of the home will become one of joy as hurtful attitudes are laid aside.

If indeed you have heard Him and have been taught by Him as the truth is in Jesus: that you put off, concerning your former conduct, the old man which grows corrupt according to the deceitful lusts, and be renewed in the spirit of your mind, and that you put on the new man which was created according to God, in true righteousness and holiness (Eph. 4:21–24).

Forgiveness and kindness will become house rules. Couples are enabled to overcome temptation with faithfulness to each other. When husbands and wives give their expectations to God and focus on the good, peace will rule in their hearts and in their home.

God gives us the power of the Holy Spirit to help believers withstand temptation. The presence of Christ becomes the couples' spiritual armor to withstand the fiery darts of Satan.

Finally, my brethren, be strong in the Lord and the power of His might. Put on the whole armor of God, that you may be able to stand against the wiles of the devil (Eph. 6:10–11).

He also extends His presence through loving and supportive fellowship with believers in the church (2 Cor. 13:11). He prepares for protection from abuses through establishing civil authorities (Rom. 13:1). There are examples in the Bible of people who understood their godly roles as husband and wife and some who did not understand their role.

Sarah stood by Abraham through good choices and bad decisions. She loved her husband unconditionally. Sarah was strong willed, but she chose to submit to Abraham. She was a dutiful wife. Her love and loyalty to Abraham was blessed by Abraham's devotion to her. He recognized her as his equal. The intensity of their union deepened and became like a mighty force that

nothing, not even Hagar, a second wife and mother of Abraham's child Ishmael, could diminish. Sarah called him lord.[2]

Calling him lord was a title of great respect.

Isaac's wife Rebekah had a lack of reverence and respect for her husband and his leadership and exhibited favoritism concerning her sons which brought into her home rivalry, deceit, and contention.

Roles of Husband and Wife

Marriage requires the commitment to carry out your responsibilities as husband or wife and to give up the selfishness partners tend to have. It is very difficult in today's society to remain focused on the individual roles of both husband and wife. The wife is told that she has the same rights as her husband. Pressure is being placed on the husband to take care of himself and not to worry about her. Husbands and wives need direction. The following are the biblical roles of husbands and wives. Memorizing and studying individual roles and Scriptures relating to roles will lead to oneness and a more harmonious family relationship and marriage.

Try giving up your needs for one week and focus solely on satisfying the needs of your spouse. Watch the response you receive when you give up your needs. Your spouse may be so surprised that he or she will immediately change his or her behavior also. If you don't see a change, pray and continue satisfying your mate.

God has different expectations for marriage:

God's perfect plan for marriage enables us to serve someone else's

Checklist for Husbands

☐ Submit to the Lord (1 Cor. 11:3).

☐ Be a leader and follow the example of Christ's love for the church (Eph. 5:25).

☐ Be head of your wife (Eph. 5:23). This does not mean to have a master-slave relationship, but a partnership. The man is the guide and leader.

☐ Dwell with your wife with understanding, giving honor to her as the weaker vessel. Respect her as your equal. Show courtesy, consideration, and emotional support. Study and learn your wife (1 Pet. 3:7).

☐ Love your wife (Eph. 5:25–33).

☐ Don't expect perfection (Eph. 4:32).

☐ Pray and depend on the Lord's instruction to learn how to love her (Col. 1:9).

☐ Minister to her and help her with her problems with understanding (Eph. 5:26–27).

☐ Consult with your wife when making decisions (Col. 3:19).

☐ Praise your wife (Prov. 31:28).

☐ Have only one wife (Mark 10:1–12).

☐ Be faithful to your wife (Prov. 5:15:20). Beware of the immoral woman. Resist temptation by removing yourself from the seductress (Prov. 5).

☐ Be a man of confidence (Phil. 4:13).

☐ Discipline your children with love and do not provoke them to wrath (Eph. 6:4; Col. 3:21).

☐ Abstain from using a sharp tongue. This makes a person feel inferior.

☐ Be gentle towards your wife, control temper, and abstain from physical violence (Rom. 13:1).

☐ Communicate with her socially, mentally, verbally, and physically (Prov. 15:1).

☐ Do not leave your wife, though unbelieving (1 Cor. 7:10–16).

☐ Be generous towards your wife. King Ahasuerus gave Queen Esther half his kingdom (Esth. 5:3).

☐ Do not interfere with your wife's duty to Christ. Other loyalties must be subordinate to the devotion to the Lord (Luke 14:26–27).

☐ Be a provider for your family (1 Tim. 5:8).

☐ Protect your wife and family (Gen. 14:14).

☐ Be a man of courage and faith (Deut. 31:6).

needs. The Apostle Paul made it clear that those who are married can expect not only the joys of the relationship but also the responsibilities that come with it. Paul indicated that in committing yourselves to one another, husbands and wives actually must spend much of their time working hard to please one another (1 Cor. 7:33–35).

If you apply the Word of God to your marriage, your marriage will change. Scripture doesn't reveal that we must make sure our life partner loves, respects, and gives us all the affection or financial and physical satisfaction we long for. The Bible never promises that God will make our mates into the kind of people we pray they should be. It does tell us, however, what kind of a heart God can enable us to have if we do our part in bringing out the best in our mate. Marriage demands spiritual growth. To live with and love

Checklist for Wives

(Place an (x) next to areas in which you need improvement)

- ❑ Submit to your own husband as to the Lord (Eph. 5:22).
- ❑ Be his helper and partner to work towards goals (Gen. 2:18).
- ❑ Encourage and support his leadership (1 Cor. 11:3).
- ❑ Love and be obedient to him (Titus 2:4–5).
- ❑ Do not nag, rather have a gentle and quiet spirit (1 Pet. 3:1–4).
- ❑ Have no dominion over man (1 Tim. 2:11–12).
- ❑ Be faithful and affectionate to husband (1 Cor. 7:2–3).
- ❑ Must not leave husband (1 Cor. 7).
- ❑ Help as a provider. First responsibility is to be home with the children (Prov. 31:24).
- ❑ Work hard to help husband build home (Prov. 14:1).
- ❑ Aged women teach the young women to be sober and to love their husbands and children (Titus 2:4).
- ❑ Must not judge her husband's leadership with criticism (Prov. 16:24) (1 Pet. 3:4).
- ❑ Must not drive her husband away (Prov. 14:1).
- ❑ Be a homemaker by keeping a clean, neat house and rise early to prepare breakfast for her family (Prov. 31:15).
- ❑ Be a good cook (Gen. 18:6, 27:9).
- ❑ Be thrifty minded when shopping for family and look for bargains. Must not be an impulsive spender (Prov. 31:14, 16 & 18, 19:14).
- ❑ Be benevolent to the poor (Prov. 31:20).
- ❑ Maintain family clothes (Acts 9:39).
- ❑ Works late into the night if necessary (Prov. 31:18).
- ❑ Do not gossip with friends and family (1 Tim. 3:11) (Prov. 10:18).
- ❑ Careful, godly appearance. Always look and smell good for your husband. (Prov. 31:17) (Song of Sol. 4:9–11).

someone else requires us to put our spouse's interests ahead of our own.

Marriage demands commitment, risk, and unselfish investment. For a couple to achieve the unity, love, loyalty, and blessing God expects, they must take giant strides towards personal growth. They must learn how and when to abandon personal rights so they can experience the richness that comes when the true needs of others (not the selfish demands) are put before their own desires.

As husbands and wives learn to love in this way, they become a window through which others can see the kingdom of God at work. As they surrender themselves to the Spirit and rule of God, they become exhibits of the kind of spirituality that God designed marriage to produce. Friends, children, and extended family are given a chance to see the kind of faithful love, honesty, moral courage, true humility, incredible patience, and tender understanding God can give in marriage. People will not see manipulative or fearful compliance that so often marks marriage. They will see honest caring and friendship. This kind of love requires us to focus not primarily on our mate's faults but on our own motives and actions.

Win your husband or wife back the same way you did when you kept that fire burning by speaking loving words towards each other when you were dating.

Couples Who Have A Strong Marriage:

1. Are committed to God.
2. Meet their emotional needs by doing for each other.
3. Do not take each other for granted.
4. Have agape love for each other.
5. Do not keep score of wrongdoing.
6. Have strong sense of commitment to the marriage covenant and are determined to make their marriages work.
7. Do not put friends and relatives before God and spouse.
8. Are strong minded. They do not lose themselves in the relationship. They form their own opinions, make decisions, and pursue goals. The wife is, however, submissive to the husband's authority in that she defers to her husband's judgment in making the final decision on what is best for the family. (Refer to the section on communication concerning the appropriate way to communicate with your spouse.)
9. Have a fulfilling sexual relationship.
10. Like to talk to each other. They spend a great deal of time sharing thoughts about different topics.

They are not manipulative or condescending. They are open and direct, and listen and respect each other's opinion.
11. Think positively during times of despair. They have faith that things will get better. They pray and put every unresolved issue in the hands of the Lord to work out.
12. Don't take blessings for granted. They recognize that everything belongs to our Lord and appreciate what they have without bragging and acting superior.
13. Express appreciation and are generous with praise.
14. Don't put each other down.
15. Are deeply spiritual and pray together. They have strong spiritual or religious convictions and commit themselves to a spiritual lifestyle.
16. Are sensitive to other people. They recognize the needs of others, respect their differences, and consider their feelings.
17. Suggest instead of giving advice.
18. Refrain from judging.

READ THE SONG OF SOLOMON TOGETHER

Solomon and Sheba confess the feelings of a lover and his beloved. "While this song dispels notions of celibacy and asceticism as an ideal, it does not presume sexual relations outside a marriage relationship."[3]

Wife   Let him kiss me with the kisses of his mouth. . . .

Husband   I have compared you, my love, to horses among Pharaoh's chariots. Your cheeks are lovely with ornaments, your neck with chains of gold.

Wife   While the king is at his table, my spikenard sends forth its fragrance. A bundle of myrrh is my beloved to me; he shall lie all night between my breasts. My beloved is unto me as a cluster of henna blooms in the vineyards of En Gedi.

Husband   Behold, you are fair, my love! Behold, you are fair! You have dove's eyes.

Wife   Behold, you are handsome, my beloved! Yes, pleasant! Also our bed is green. The beams of our houses are cedar, and our rafters of fir. I am the rose of Sharon, and the lily of the valleys.

Loving Relationships:

How To Put the Love Back in Your Relationship

Hug and touch each other frequently.

Greet each other at the door.

Compliment each other often.

Do things you did when you were dating.

Send a card or love note to your spouse.

Send flowers.

Telephone to say I love you during the day.

Telephone when you don't have anything specific to talk about.

Listen attentively.

Think about what pleases your spouse and act on it.

Talk about positive memories.

Spend quality time together.

Make a date often.

Vacation together without the kids.

Assure your spouse often that you care.

Show that you care through your actions.

Make your spouse priority number two after your relationship with God.

Children, family, and friends should not be placed above your relationship to your husband.

Thank your partner for compliments and kind gestures and you'll get more of them.

Get rid of anger, resentment, and bitterness quickly.

Practice forgiveness always.

Think about the other person's feelings.

Pray together.

Have fun together. Think of something you do that the two of you enjoy doing together alone.

Look for the good in your partner.

Admire each other's achievements.

Think about the things that made you fall in love in the first place.

Have candlelight dinners.

Always make your partner feel special when you are alone and also around others.

Husband   Like a lily among thorns, so is my love among the daughters.

Wife   Like an apple tree among the trees of the woods, so is my beloved among the sons. I sat down in his shade with great delight, and his fruit was sweet to my taste. He brought me to the banqueting house, and his banner over me was love. Sustain me with cakes of raisins, refresh me with apples, for I am lovesick. His left hand is under my head, and his right hand embraces me. . . .

The voice of my beloved! Behold, he comes leaping upon the mountains, skipping upon the hills. My beloved is like a gazelle or a young stag. Behold, he stands behind our wall; he is looking through the windows, gazing through the lattice. My beloved spoke, and said to me: "Rise up, my love, my fair one, and come away. For lo, the winter is past, the rain is over and gone. The flowers appear on the earth; the time of singing has come, and the voice of the turtledove is heard in our land. The fig tree puts forth her green figs, and the vines with the tender grapes give a good smell. Rise up my love, my fair one, and come away! O my dove, in the clefts of the rock, in the secret places of the cliff, let me see your face, let me hear your voice. For your voice is sweet, and your face is lovely." . . . My beloved is mine, and I am his. He feeds his flock among the lilies.

Husband   Behold, you are fair, my love! Behold, you are fair! You have dove's eyes behind your veil. Your hair is like a flock of goats, going down from Mount Gilead. Your teeth are like a flock of shorn sheep which have come up from the washing, every one of which bears twins, and none is barren among them. Your lips are like a strand of scarlet, and your mouth is lovely. Your temples behind your veil are like a piece of pomegranate. Your neck is like the tower of David, built for an armory, on which hang a thousand bucklers, all shields of mighty men. Your two breasts are like two fawns, twins of a gazelle, which feed among the lilies. . . . You are all fair, my love, and there is no spot in you. Come with me from Lebanon, my spouse. . . . You have ravished my heart, . . . with one look of your eyes, with one link of your necklace. How fair is your love, my sister, my spouse! How much better than wine is your love, and the scent of your perfumes than all spices! And the scent of perfumes than all spices! Your lips, O my spouse, drip as the honeycomb; honey and milk are under your tongue; and the fragrance of your garments is like the fragrance of Lebanon. . . . Your plants are an orchard of pomegranates with pleasant fruits, fragrant henna with spikenard, spikenard and saffron, calamus and cinnamon, with all trees of frankincense, myrrh and aloes, with all the chief spices. . . .

Wife   I have taken off my robe; how can I put it on again? I have washed my feet; how can I defile them? My beloved put his hand by the latch of the door, and my heart yearned for him. I arose to open for my beloved, and my hands dripped with myrrh, my fingers with liquid myrrh, on the handles of the lock. . . .

Husband   O my love, you are as beautiful as Tirzah, lovely as Jerusalem, awesome as an army with banners! Turn your eyes away from me. Your hair is like a flock of goats going down from Gilead. Your teeth are like a flock of sheep which have come up from the washing. . . . There are sixty queens and eighty concubines, and virgins without number. My dove, my perfect one, is the only one. . . .

How beautiful are your feet in sandals, the curves of your thighs are like jewels, your navel is a rounded goblet which lacks no blended beverage. Your waist is a heap of wheat set about with lilies. Your neck is like an ivory tower, your eyes like the pools in Heshbon by the gate of Bath Rabbim. Your nose is like the tower of Lebanon which looks toward Damascus. Your head crowns you like Mount Carmel, and the hair of your head is like purple; the king is held captive by its tresses. How fair and how pleasant you are, O love, with your delights! This stature of yours is like a palm tree, and your breasts like its clusters. I said, "I will go up to the palm tree, I will take hold if its branches. . . . "

Wife   I am my beloved's, and his desire is toward me. Come, my beloved, let us go forth to the field; let us lodge in the villages. . . . There I will give you my love. The mandrakes give off a fragrance. . . .

Set me as a seal upon your heart, as a seal upon your arm; for love is as strong as death. . . . Many waters cannot quench love, nor can the floods drown it.

Chapter 7

Children Are a Heritage

"And whoever receives one little child like this in my name, receives me." —Matthew 18:5

All children are gifts from God. We are all God's children whether we are someone's biological child, adopted child, or stepchild. We should accept children like Jesus Christ has accepted us. If God assigns parents the responsibility to raise His children, then why do some people have difficulty raising children whom they feel are someone's else's responsibility? Whatever your situation is at this time in your life, it is part of God's plan for you to raise the children that are in your family. Learn from examples in the Bible such as Joseph, who gladly accepted Jesus, providing Him with all the love, encouragement, guidance, and training that a son needs from a father. Although Eli had problems with his sons, he gladly accepted Samuel after Hannah gave him to the Lord (1 Sam. 1:11, 25).

Then Israel saw Joseph's sons, and said, "Who are these?" And Joseph said to his father, "They are my sons, whom God has given me in this place." And he said, "Please bring them to me, and I will bless them" (Gen. 48:8–9).

The Bible makes it clear that God the giver of life, having made us in His image and likeness, intends for us to be fruitful and increase in number.

Children are the Lord's special blessing.

Behold, children are a heritage from the Lord, the fruit of the womb is His reward. Like arrows in the hand of a warrior, so are the children of one's youth. Happy is the man who has his quiver full of them; they shall not be ashamed, but shall speak with their enemies in the gate (Ps. 127:3–5).

Jesus saw greatness in children.

At the time the disciples came to Jesus, saying, "Who then is greatest in the kingdom of heaven?" And Jesus called a little child to Him, set him in the midst of them, and said, "Assuredly, I say to you, unless you are converted and become as little children, you will by no means enter the kingdom of heaven. Therefore whoever humbles himself as this little child is the greatest in the kingdom of heaven. And whoever receives one little child like this in My name receives Me. But whoever causes one of these little ones who believe in Me to sin, it would be better for him if a millstone were hung around his neck and he were drowned in the depth of the sea" (Matt. 18:1–6).

He also intends for parents to teach children the ways of God.

Gather the people together, men and women and little ones, and the stranger who is within your gates, that they may hear and that they may learn to fear the Lord your God and carefully observe all the words of this law, and that their children, who have not known it, may hear and learn to fear the Lord your God as long as you live . . . (Deut. 31:12–13).

God assigns parents the awesome task and responsibility of raising children. Whether you are a stepparent or biological parent your responsibility is to raise children based on Scriptural principles, teaching them godly ways.

Grief, Separation, Divorce, and Loyalty Issues

When we make decisions for ourselves, we sometimes forget the impact these decisions will have on our children. Because of the selfish nature we are all born with we make decisions we feel are in our best interest, and we don't consider the children. In the case of divorce, "The disruption and discord surrounding divorce almost always adversely affect the children for at least a year or two. Immediately before and after divorce, children show signs of emotional pain, such as depression or rebellion, and symptoms of stress such as anger, low school achievement, poor health, and few friends. Whether this distress is relatively mild and short-lived or serious and long-lasting depends primarily on the stability of the child's life and the adequacy of the caregiving arrangement."[1]

Since these emotional signs may surface in children of stepfamilies, the biological parent in the home may be aware of these signs and react in a very over protective and sometimes overly sensitive way. It is important that parents make a special effort to minister to the needs of children who are in this unique family structure. These children enter blended families with a history of loss and change that is beyond their control. They may have experienced their parents's troubled marriage/relationship or a parent's death.

Children may believe that acceptance of a new stepparent will mean they are betraying the absent biological parent. They may fear that expressing pleasure in the blended family is in some way showing disloyalty to the absent parent. The initial rejection of a stepparent may have nothing to do with the personal characteristics of that person, but may reflect a loyalty struggle going on within the child. Powerless, these children are forced to adjust to changes in the new situation with stepparents and stepsiblings that they are not emotionally ready for. This can be very confusing for children. They tend to blame themselves and manifest guilt and shame for what happened. Children often become fearful that all relationships will end in failure. Children are torn between the parents they live with and the parent who lives somewhere else. Adopted and foster children experience an additional loss, which compounds the feelings of rejection.

The most apparent reason is that two adults, both of whom have known and loved the child since birth, generally provide more complete care than one. Not only can a mother and father together be given an extra measure of the warmth, discipline, and attention that all children need, but they can also support each other, provide respite for each other, and try to compensate for each other's parental shortcomings and enhance each other's parental strengths. Children who live with both biological parents develop a deep sense of commitment to family, especially to their parents who have taught them from birth to love and respect them.

When couples consider separating or divorcing they often believe that children can readily accept change and that they tend to be resilient and can in some way bounce back quickly.

> Children are swept into the turbulence of divorce or death and the drastic changes that follow. Then they experience the dating and remarriage of their parents. They have no control over many of these events that are having a major effect on their lives, and they feel helpless and angry. While it is likely that children are more flexible than adults, their adjustment depends on how well they are helped through this chaotic time. For the parent and stepparent to have a good relationship with their child, they must recognize and understand the child's feelings and what motivates his or her behavior.[2]

It will take time for children to find their place in the new family, feel secure, and realize that there is enough love to go around.

Stability in the child's life is an important factor in determining the ease or difficulty of divorce or separation for children. Visitation is essential for maintaining connectedness.

> The most destructive source and a major source of instability is open hostility between the child's parents, especially if one parent threatens to harm the other. Unfortunately, even when the reason for divorce is to end long-standing hostility, marital break-up itself is usually characterized by an escalation of conflict. Many divorcing parents yell insults, exchange blows, destroy each other's property, or undermine each other's dignity and equanimity with greater intensity than ever before.[3]

> Another major source of instability is the child's being separated completely from a caregiver to which he or she is highly attached. Non-custodial parents tend to visit their offspring less frequently and more inconsistently over time and their children miss them.[4]

Children may experience feelings of fear, helplessness, depression, suspicion, and rejection during the initial stage of remarriage. These feelings are to be expected. Children need reassurance and specific information about what changes will take place in their lives. Separation brings about sad feelings in children. In most cases, children are very attached to biological parents. A child's identity comes from his or her mother and father, creating a strong attachment to both parents.

> A child's security, or lack of it, depends upon their feeling of acceptance and having a place within the family. Children form views, opinions and behaviors that reflect their family's outlook. They absorb their family's values, beliefs, and convictions and try to fit within the family pattern. When a stepfamily is formed, many of the old views, values and rules are dismissed and family members must adjust to a new set of ideas and rules. Children cannot simply wipe away the years of personal development and immediately become different people just because they are now stepchildren in a new family.[5]

Parents must be sensitive to the feelings of loss that children frequently experience in blended families. Blended families should be aware that children must be allowed time to mourn their loss. There are many feelings that surface in children. They may be angry with the custodial parents because they had to move away from the absent biological parent. They may be angry with the absent parent because he or she does not call or want to visit with them frequently.

Facing these issues with children may be difficult and stressful. Negative behavior is not always the result of hatred or personal differences. Children may vent their anger upon family members. We faced the challenge of dealing with anger in our youngest son who had a very difficult time handling separation issues. After my separation and subsequent divorce from my first husband, my children and I lived together for a few years prior to my remarriage to my current husband. My son was a preschooler who was very close to me. He would leave his bed every night and get into my bed in the middle of the night. After I married my husband, my children had to share me with this stranger whom they did not know. This affected my son who could no longer sleep in mommy's bed. He felt this person somehow interfered with our relationship. His anger was manifested in ways that were very stressful for our family. We sought help immediately when we could no longer handle his outbursts of anger. One of the ways we helped our son was by each of us spending quality time with him alone to allow him to discuss his feelings. We also felt this was necessary to help my husband build a relationship with him to help strengthen their bond. Our son improved over time.

The best situation for a child after a divorce is one in which parents can cooperate amiably on the child's behalf and in which the child can continue an intimate, positive relationship with each parent. This is particularly true if the custodial parent provides both warmth and a stable structure for the child's daily life, and the non-custodial parent provides the child with ongoing support, psychological as well as financial.[6]

Parents must immediately address the child's feelings of guilt. Discuss the changes and provide them with direct, non-judgmental, non-critical information about the situation. Be open to listening to your child's concerns. The message should be clear to the child, "you did nothing wrong."

What's in a Name

It is sometimes difficult for stepparents and children to decide what children should call the new parent. The parents and children should decide on what the stepparent should be called. Some stepparents are comfortable with children using their first name, however, others may be uncomfortable with this and believe it is disrespectful to call an adult by his or her first name. However, adult children may be uncomfortable calling a stepparent Mom or Dad. The title Mr. or Mrs. is too formal. Parents should discuss this with the children and decide what the children should call the stepparent.

Beware of Favoritism and Partiality

Children feel the pain when one parent favors one child over another. This can be very emotionally harmful to children. There are examples in the Bible of parents who favored one child over another. Favoritism causes conflict between the parents and jealousy between siblings.

"I charge you before God and the Lord Jesus Christ and the elect angels that you observe these things without prejudice, doing nothing with partiality" (1 Tim. 5:21).

"But when his brothers saw that their father loved him more than all his brothers, they hated him and could not speak peacably to him" (Gen. 37:4).

Bonding with Stepparent

It is important that a strong relationship develop between stepparent and stepchild. Gradually develop the relationship by spending time with each child. Stepparents can promote bonding by following the guidelines in the section in this book on "The Roles of Stepparents."

Visiting Children

Visiting children usually feel very different in unfamiliar surroundings. Families must make these children feel as welcomed and as comfortable as possible. Visiting children should have a place in the household that is their own. For example: a drawer, a shelf for toys or clothes or a bedroom if there are enough rooms in the home. Include stepchildren in family chores, projects, and activities. This will make them feel more connected to the group. Have them bring friends over when they come to visit. Children should feel safe and comfortable at both residences.

Sibling Bonding

Close sibling relationships must be promoted. Brothers and sisters usually play well together, and sometimes they fight. Sibling rivalry is very common. In stepfamilies rivalry can be more intense. We expect the children to get along and have fun together. In our minds, we feel children like to have other children around to play with. We again expect the children to feel as we do in the new family, "We will be one big happy family." Remember how well the Brady kids blended together? The reality is that

Stepsiblings rarely feel close to one another in the beginning. Often the only thing they have in common is that their parents are married to each other. Many times young members of blended families feel overwhelmed in the wake of their parents' decision to start a new family. While their parents are enjoying a new relationship, the children in blended families are re-establishing themselves, from sharing rooms to sharing pets, and adjusting to new stepsiblings.[7]

The marriage relationship will set the tone for bonding of sibling relationships. Parents must promote open communication among the siblings to help them bond.

The arrival of a new sibling often helps to bond all members of the family.

> The baby provides a link for the step-family. For the first time, the members of the blended family will be related by blood and history. Whether this new link will strengthen or weaken the stepfamily's emotional bond depends partly on the reasons for having the baby and how the family adjusts to the new member.[8]

The arrival of our daughter strengthened the bond between the stepsiblings. They now have a half–sister that provided the needed link. However, "the new sibling may spark old feelings of desertion and anger in children from the parents' former marriages. The attention a half-sibling receives often reminds visiting stepsiblings of how little time their natural parents have to share with them. This especially seems true if the new half-sibling arrives before the blended family members have adjusted to their new lifestyle."[9]

Ages of Children and Bonding

In blended families it takes time to bond with children who are not biologically related to the stepparent. Couples tend to immediately expect instant bonding and loyalty from the children. It also takes time to build up a sense of loyalty, and for some children it can take many years. Couples are encouraged to not be overbearing with children and to take things slowly. Look for activities that promote bonding between adults and children. Keep in mind that children have loyalty issues they are dealing with.

Infant and Preschool Children

Young children tend to adjust quickly and easily to change; however, they experience a sense of displacement and will react to changes and disruptions in the family. Young children also experience stresses relating to separation issues. As the new parents comfort and spend time with the young child, they will grow close and symptoms will disappear. Physical care is the primary route to parent-child bonding in the early years. As the child grows older, less physical care will be needed. The child will crave attention in other areas.

School-Age Children and Adolescents

Integrating a stepfamily that contains school-age children and teenagers can be difficult. The more years the child spends with the biological parents, the stronger the bond and the harder it is for children to adjust to a change in circumstances. Not only do parents have to contend with loyalty issues but they also have to contend with behaviors connected with growth and development, particularly when dealing with teenagers. Mark Twain put it this way, "When a child turns 13, you put him in a barrel with only a hole to feed him through. When he turns 18, plug the hole." Parents of teenagers understand the challenges of raising teenagers and dealing with their issues. Adolescents move away from their families emotionally in any type of family to form their own identity. Their need for independence can run counter to the needs of a family. In a blended family, it is important that all parents work closely to establish consistent rules for teenagers during these formative years. According to adolescent mental health specialists, a young person will experience the feeling of being torn between the parents he or she lives with and the divorced parent who lives somewhere else. In some cases, teens manipulate parents to get their way.

In single-parent families, teenagers have often been required to take on adult responsibilities and when marriage or remarriage of the parent occurs, the child often finds it extremely difficult or even impossible to return to the role of being a child.

Stepparents should find activities that allow a close parent/child relationship to develop. If the stepparent and the child share an interest, there are more opportunities for bonding. A stepmother and stepchild may both like to garden. A stepfather and stepchild may like basketball or golf.

Adult Children

Couples must agree on how to deal with adult children. Change for adult children is more difficult for them to handle. Their history of life experiences has already been established. The difficulty in adjusting is not because they do not like the stepparent, but because of these lifelong experiences, they often have a difficult time adjusting to the new arrangement. If a couple encounters a situation where the adult stepchild refuses to accept the new arrangement, the biological parent can only demand that the stepchild respect the stepparent. Most adult stepchildren feel less obligated to be fully involved in family activities because they are living independent lives of their own. If you are in a situation where the adult child refuses to accept your new situation and refuses to communicate with you, pray for your adult child. Jesus provided a pattern for a healthy relationship between adult

children and their parents when a child is lost. Read the story about the prodigal son in Luke 15. The loving bond between parent and child should not be broken by aging, transfer of residence, or changes in circumstances. Rather, it should remain as an enduring commitment between parents and offspring from birth to death to be available to each other and responsive to each other's needs.

> When I was my father's son, tender and the only one in the sight of my mother, he also taught me, and said to me: Let your heart retain my words; keep my commands, and live. Get wisdom! Get Understanding! Do not forget, nor turn away from the words of my mouth (Prov. 4:3–5).

Adopted Children

Adopted children are the chosen children. We include this section on adoption because we feel very strongly about adopting children. Adoption is assuming parental responsibility for the child of another. There are people in the Bible who adopted children. Moses was adopted by Pharaoh's daughter (Exod. 2:1–10). His adoption, though sad for his Israelite parents, was part of God's plan for the deliverance of Israel from Egypt. Mordecai adopted his young relative Esther after the death of her parents (Esth. 2:7). The Bible presents adoption as a positive gracious act that is part of God's plan.

Adoption is the means by which all believers enter into the family of God.

> So also, when we were children, we were in slavery under the basic principles of the world. But when the time had fully come, God sent his Son, born of a woman, born under law, to redeem those under law, that

we might receive the full rights of sons. Because you are sons, God sent the Spirit of his Son into our hearts, the Spirit who calls out, Abba Father. So you are no longer a slave, but a son; and since you are a son, God has made you also an heir (Gal. 4:3–7 NIV).

When is Outside Counseling Necessary?

According to the Center for Adolescent Health Fact Sheets, the following are signs that would suggest the need for outside help:

When the child cannot seem to control his or her anger and it affects his home and school performance.

When the family is affected by the stress.

When members of the family get no enjoyment from normally pleasurable activities.

Professional counseling should be sought if families are unable to handle conflicts. God's word, in Matt. 18:14–18 instructs us to seek counsel when we are not able to handle situations ourselves.

In the same way your Father in heaven is not willing that any of these little ones should be lost. If your brother sins against you, go and show him his fault, just between the two of you. If he listens to you, you have won your brother over. But if he will not listen, take one or two others along, so that "every matter may be established by the testimony of two or three witnesses." If he refuses to listen to them, tell it to the church; and if he refuses to listen

Stresses for Children in Stepfamilies

1. Hearing their biological parents argue and say negative things to each other. Kids tend to blame themselves.
2. Not being able or allowed to see their absent parent and resenting their custodial parents.
3. Feeling abandoned by a parent.
4. Not communicating with absent parent.
5. Not visiting absent parent.
6. Feeling they are to blame for everything.
7. Fear that their current family will break up.
8. Having their parents do more for stepsiblings than for them.
9. Having stepsiblings get into their belongings and intrude on their space and privacy.
10. Dealing with feelings of not being wanted.
11. Feeling angry and depressed and wishing it could all be the way it was before the death or divorce.
12. Having a stepparent tell them what to do and resenting the new authority figure in the household.
13. Feeling like pawns and messengers tossed between their biological parents who are still feeling bitter and angry towards each other.
14. Adjusting to all the new rules in the household.
15. The feeling of being different from other children because they are not part of what they feel is a real family.

even to the church, treat him as you would a pagan or a tax collector.

All children should be given the encouragement, praise, structure, and affirmation that builds the security that a family provides.

Chapter 8

What We Can Do To Help Our Blended Families

"Behold, how good and how pleasant it is for brethren to dwell together in unity!" —Psalm 133:1

This chapter provides spiritual guidance on how to achieve and maintain harmonious relationships within the family. As we have indicated throughout this book, the Bible is our blueprint for living and for successful marriage and family relationships. The Bible does not specifically address the issue of blended families; however, it gives us admonitions that are relevant.

The godly purpose of the family is to provide emotional, financial, and spiritual support for its members. The family unit was established by God as a part of His perfect plan for marriage, and His instructions to couples were to go forth, be fruitful, and multiply. For many years, psychologists and other professionals were not interested in blended families. Consequently, stepfamilies were on their own in developing parenting strategies. This is changing. Still, what research reveals can be discouraging for stepfamilies. It is becoming obvious that blended families have to work very hard to accomplish unity.

For the stepfamily, survival depends on facing reality and handling it with prayer, love, wisdom, and patience.

The blended family, either by circumstance or by choice, has been given God's abundant grace.

There are qualities that exist in blended families that do not exist in traditional families; however, these families can live by the godly principles taught to traditional families. The benefits of these unique families are that they have the opportunity to share new skills and interests with each other, learn new customs and rituals, and have a more diverse companionship within the household that does not exist in traditional families. This chapter will discuss what you can expect from this type of family and provide you with solutions on how to correct problems that may already exist or will likely occur. The goal is to achieve the rewarding relationships, intimacy, commitment, and security that members within the family desire.

Before we begin addressing the solutions, we would like to discuss what happened to John and Kathy's relationship as a result of counseling. John and Kathy sought Christian counseling as we indicated in the beginning of the book. Prior to the counseling sessions, they were not knowledgeable about the Word of God. Although they attended church and Sunday School when they were children, like many of us as we became young adults, they departed from the church and began to live a worldly life. However, their friends were so convincing in their witnessing to them that they decided they would seek Christian counseling. After six months of counseling, John and Kathy gained a new revelation about God's perfect plan for marriage.

At their first session, John and Kathy learned about how Jesus Christ died on the cross for their sins. They were told about the plan of salvation. The only thing they did not understand at the time was how all of this would help their marriage and family. The counselor discussed God's perfect plan for marriage, and discussed how past hurt and pain can negatively impact a new marriage if not addressed. They read Scripture together. After the first session, John and Kathy were surprised about the extent of knowledge in the Word of God and how these Scriptures can be applied to everyday life. They joined a church and accepted Jesus Christ as their personal savior. They experienced a hunger to learn more about the Word of God. They joined the married couples' ministry in their church and they decided to have family worship at home. The kids attended Sunday school and they all began studying the Bible together.

John and Kathy began experiencing changes in their marriage as they focused on their individual spiritual growth. After four counseling sessions, John and Kathy knew that the mighty power of God through the Holy Spirit was healing their marriage and family. They now understand the disillusionment they experienced in their marriage. They realized through Scripture study that they did not marry the wrong person. They began praying together and studying what their individual roles should be as husband and wife. John and Kathy realized they had been inclined towards their own selfishness in their relationship with each other. Soon, John and Kathy did not need counseling any longer, their marriage changed, and their relationship changed as they experienced the blessings of the Lord Jesus Christ.

To combat the challenges in the blended family, John and Kathy's family as well as other families must have a Christ-centered home. Harmony and peace will result if the family is growing together spiritually, praying, and studying the Word of God.

Blended families can live by the godly principles taught to couples who are in traditional marriages. Blended families that are established as a result of divorce and remarriage must be ministered to by giving them support, encouragement, comfort, and teaching just as the drug addict, murderer, fornicator, adulterer, and other sinners are ministered to. Churches must address the burdens of broken families.

Pure and undefiled religion before God and the Father is this: to visit orphans and widows in their trouble, and to keep oneself unspotted from the world (James 1:27).

The purpose of the ministry to blended families is to not condone divorce and remarriage but to minister forgiveness and healing to these families and to address biblically the unique issues and challenges these families face. We strongly encourage people who are in traditional marriage to stay together. God will bless your marriage if you seek him.

It is also necessary to minister to blended families who are formed as a result of death of a spouse, marriage of a single parent, adoption, or foster parenting. The purpose of the ministry must be to address biblically the unique issues these families face.

Blended Families in the Bible

There are many examples in the Bible of blended families, which were referred to as extended families during this time.

Abraham and Sarah were an example of a couple whose family shifted from a traditional family to a blended family. This family experienced conflict and contention as a result of not waiting patiently on the Lord for their blessing. This story is also an example of how outside influences can cause conflict in the home. Abraham was a man of faith and God recognized his faith. God made a covenant with Abraham and promised him that he would be the father of a great nation and that he would have an heir. The Lord said to Abraham,

On the same day the Lord made a covenant with Abram, saying: "To your descendants I have given this land, from the river of Egypt to the great river" . . . (Gen. 15:18).

Sarah, Abraham's wife, had given him no children by the age of 76. She asked Abraham to go to her Egyptian maidservant Hagar. Sarah thought she could have a family through her maidservant. (This was the custom during this time,

but a clear violation of God's law). Abraham did as Sarah said. Sarah in an unselfish act took Hagar and gave her to Abraham for his wife. Sarah believed she was not the chosen one to have his child and she wanted to bring about God's promise. After Hagar became pregnant, Sarah said to Abraham, "May my wrong be on you! I gave you my servant for your wife and when she saw she was with child, she no longer had respect for me." During her pregnancy, Hagar began to despise Sarah and act very proud, and Sarah became jealous. Hagar was proud because she believed she had been promoted by Sarah to the status of second wife. When Sarah complained to Abraham, he told her to do whatever she wanted with Hagar. When Sarah acted cruelly towards her, Hagar ran away.[1]

Earthly choices bring about bitter consequences. Abraham was 86 years old when Hagar gave birth to Ishmael. An angel of the Lord appeared to Hagar and told her to return to her mistress and to be submissive to her. Sarah eventually formed an attachment to Ishmael. Years later, when Abraham was 100 years old and Sarah 90, Sarah gave birth to Isaac. Isaac had a very gentle spirit, which was in contrast to the aggressive spirit of Ishmael. On one of Isaac's birthdays, his father celebrated his weaning by having a feast. Hagar and Ishmael stood outside mocking. Once again Sarah wanted them cast out. She did not want Ishmael to be heir with Isaac. Sarah did not want to raise Isaac with an aggressive half-brother and his jealous mother. Sarah appeared wise in making this decision.

And the matter was very displeasing in Abraham's sight because of his son. But God said to Abraham, "Let it not be grievous in thy sight because of the lad, and because of the bondwoman. In all that Sarah has said unto you, hearken to her voice; for in Isaac shall your seed be called" (Gen. 21:11–12).

Abraham sent Hagar and Ishmael away. He turned her away because of her treatment towards his wife. Hagar gained strength from God. Sarah wanted to instruct her son Isaac in wisdom without the mocking of Hagar. She was protecting her child.

Even though there were issues in Abraham's family, Abraham was a leader in his home. He taught his family and extended family and servants the Word of God. God knew that Abraham would teach his household as he instructed him to do.

> For I have known him, in order that he may command his children and his household after him that they keep the way of the Lord, to do righteousness and justice, that the Lord may bring to Abraham what He has spoken to him (Gen. 18:19).

The story of Elkanah, Hannah, and Peninnah is an example of contention in another blended family. During these polygamous times, Elkanah had two wives—Hannah and Peninnah. Peninnah had children and Hannah did not. Peninnah, her rival, would provoke her severely to make her miserable because the Lord had closed her womb. Hannah would pray for a child annually at the Temple at Shiloh. Hannah did not take revenge on her. She continued to pray each year at Shiloh. She wept and would not eat (1 Sam. 1:7). One year, she made a vow to the Lord that she would give the child back to him if he would open her womb (1 Sam. 1:11). The Lord opened Hannah's womb and she conveived Samuel. After the child was weaned, Hannah returned to the Temple to leave the child with Eli the priest. Eli accepted the responsibility of raising Hannah's child before the Lord. Eli's sons were corrupt. He did not teach his sons the ways of the Lord; however, Hannah had no fears for her son for she had faith in God.

There are many such stories in the Bible of blended/extended families, of the trials and tribulations that they endured. The one thing we have learned is that those who have an abiding faith in God, no matter what their family makeup is, can and do receive the blessings of the Father and they do find peace and harmony within their families.

All families go through trials and tribulations from time to time, but it is the character (Christlike) of the family unit that determines how the family will weather these turbulent times.

As we have stated throughout this book, it is our desire to help point blended families in the direction that will help lead them to peace and harmony. As you continue to read the latter half of this book you will hopefully be encouraged by some of the solutions that we have identified. Some may work for your family and some may not; there may be solutions that you have come up with that you want to share with us and with others. We encourage this and will make the solutions available to all. There are too many blended families in this world today to not be ministered to, especially based on the uniqueness of their situation. We have found that the Bible can indeed minister to the need of this family structure.

COMMITMENT

Into your hand I commit my spirit; You have redeemed me, O Lord God of truth (Ps. 31:5).

Commitment is defined in the American Heritage Dictionary of the

English Language as, "the act of committing; a giving in charge or entrusting; a pledge to do something; the state of being bound emotionally or intellectually to some course of action."[2]

Commitment is the foundation upon which a relationship is built, vital to its success, and an important quality of a strong family. Loving relationships grow out of commitment to our Lord Jesus Christ. Commitment requires a decision, an act of will, time, and energy. Commitment is the fundamental building block in a sound marriage and family. The marriage vow is the expression of lifelong commitment, a commitment of being in the relationship through its ups and downs. The marriage vow is a promise of lifelong commitment to your spouse. Being committed means being faithful to God and to your mate during good times and bad. Solomon and Sheba committed themselves wholly to each other.

"I am my beloved's and my beloved is mine" (Song of Sol. 6:3).

Parents must be committed to raising and teaching their children.

"Train up a child in the way he should go, and when he is old he will not depart from it" (Prov. 22:6).

In the Bible, Ruth was a woman who made a strong statement about commitment. Ruth was committed to God and to her mother-in-law Naomi. After Ruth's husband died, Naomi told her to turn back to her mother's house—a home that did not worship The Lord God of Israel. Ruth clung to her, and they traveled from Moab to Bethlehem together. Ruth said to Naomi,

Entreat me not to leave you, or to turn back from following after you;

For wherever you go, I will go; And wherever you lodge, I will lodge; Your people shall be my people, and your God, my God. Where you die, I will die, and there will I be buried. The Lord do so to me, and more also, if anything but death parts you and me (Ruth 1:16–17).

Ruth performed menial tasks to support both of them. Ruth was a very humble person with a gentle spirit who loved her mother-in-law. Ruth eventually met and married Boaz, and gave birth to a son named Obed. This blended family lived together and Naomi cared for her grandchild. Obed was the father of Jesse, who is the father of King David.

Ruth willingly accepted an unsettling future and bound herself by a solemn oath to Naomi and God. This type of commitment was a permanent bonding and the molding of hearts that linked lives that extended beyond just friendship.

When you are committed to God, you must make the choice that your family will serve the Lord, your marriage will be built on a solid foundation according to God's principles, and your children will be taught godly principles.

The Word of God will guide you towards what true commitment is. If you read and understand God's Holy Word, you will realize that commitment is achieved by undying faith in your heart for Jesus Christ.

Now therefore, fear the Lord, serve Him in sincerity and in truth . . . (Josh. 24:14).

And we know that all things work together for good to those who love God, to those who are the called according to His purpose (Rom. 8:28).

Do not be afraid of commitment, but embrace it just as Jesus Christ has embraced you.

Promoting Peace and Harmony in the Home

Finally, brethren, farewell. Become complete. Be of good comfort, be of one mind, live in peace; and the God of love and peace will be with you (2 Cor. 13:11).

Traditional and blended families must unite and work towards promoting peaceful and harmonious relationships within the family unit. Uniting, building, and strengthening relationships within the blended family may take time. These families have histories of broken promises which make it difficult for these individuals to trust. They have built protective walls or barriers around themselves. The family must make a conscious effort to strengthen the marriage bond as well as the parent-child bond.

What is a Family

In this book, we use the terms *traditional family* and *blended family*, which are both terms we use in today's society. A family—whether it is traditional, blended, nuclear, foster, or adopted—is a system of human relationships. During Old Testament times, the family was considered the "life center" of the members and the nucleus about which the sub-tribe was built. Though every effort was expended to preserve the stability of the family, tensions existed, and the Bible makes no effort to conceal them. In many families in the Bible, there were times of disharmony and no peace. Abraham quarreled with his nephew Lot (Gen. 13:5–8).

Esau disliked Jacob and Rebekah favored Jacob (Gen. 27:41, 25:28, and 27:15–17).

In a polygamous environment the only bond between siblings born to different mothers was the often remote father. At times, bitterness developed between women such as Hannah and Penninah, both wives of Elkanah. The story of Joseph's sale into Egyptian bondage (Gen. 37:12–36) vividly portrays how competition between wives in childbearing could be transmitted to the children (Gen. 30:1–7). The function of the family during this era was to maintain an atmosphere of emotional warmth and stability for rearing children. The harmony of the home was necessary to provide a stable environment for its functions.

Accordingly, in the Mosaic legislation a number of provisions were made to ensure this harmony and to circumvent rivalries that would endanger it and cause the home to break apart. A case in point may be seen in the command to honor your father and mother with the death penalty prescribed for anyone who attacked or belittled his father or his mother (Exod. 20:12 and 21:15, 17). Another effort to promote harmony in the family was the law forbidding marriage of sisters to the same husband (Lev. 18:18), an obvious effort to avoid the sort of strife that had infected Jacob's household.[3]

Strife is to be avoided because it is destructive to the family's inner cohesiveness. Any rebellion against the structure of the family must be avoided and is forbidden because of its destructive effects on the home, the fragmentation it yields, and the alienation that follows.

Every kingdom divided against itself is brought to desolation, and every city or house divided against itself will not stand (Matt. 12:25).

"The New Testament has much less to say about the family as a sociological unit. While not denying the value of strong internal ties (Luke 1:17) Jesus would not permit such ties to stand in the way of your decision to follow him (Matt. 10:3–36)."[4] However, the Scriptures indicating the close bond between husband and wife which supports a strong family bond are clear. (Eph. 5:31).

The home should be a pleasant, warm, and loving family atmosphere, which includes shared activities, a sense of kinship, expression of appreciation, family values, and family worship. Parents should extend the unconditional love they have for each other to the children. If the family is harmonious and offers stability, love, and godly guidance, the children in that family are likely to thrive. If there is peace and harmony in the family, the marriage will also thrive. The atmosphere in the home will either promote bonding in the blended family or it will cause families to tear apart. Development of a harmonious family takes time, patience, and effort.

Let all things be done decently and in order (1 Cor. 14:40).
Can two walk together unless they are agreed? (Amos 3:3).
Now I plead with you, brethren, by the name of our Lord Jesus Christ, that you all speak the same thing, and that there be no divisions among you, but that you be perfectly joined together in the same mind and in the same judgment (1 Cor. 1:10).

Walls of protection must surround the home. God has given us the responsibility to be watchmen for our homes. We are to guard our families against disturbers of peace.

We have stated in previous chapters that it is important for couples to spend quality time together. It is also important for families to spend a great deal of time together. This can be very difficult in today's society because family members spend more time away from home than they do at home. Short-term and long term planning is important to incorporate mutually satisfying activities in the family's busy schedule.

Our family reached a point where we were all so involved in individual activities that we did not have time to do things together as a family. The children would visit friends and relatives and were involved in many social activities. Edward and I would find time to spend together, but we, too, were involved in many activities. We were all so busy that our weekly family night had slipped away from us without our even knowing. We realized that we had become so busy that we did not have time for family activities. We decided to reduce the number of activities we were all involved in, and we began planning more family activities. Your family should be your number one priority in terms of how you spend your time.

Dr. Donald Joy, professor of human development writes, "The perfect vision of perfect love in human relationships is a dream worth pursuing. Whether most of us achieve it at the level we want is less important than that it hangs out there as God's target toward which we aspire."[5]

God, who has created all things good, Can make all things new, through Jesus!

COMMUNICATION

Communication is the exchange of ideas by talking or writing.

Is there Peace and Harmony in Your Home?

(Put an (X) in the area(s) in which you may need improvement)

❑ My family studies the Word of God and we work through problems

❑ We have a strong marital bond.

❑ We have a strong parent-child bond (includes biological and stepparents).

❑ We have accepted our circumstances.

❑ We have resolved hurt and pain by communicating with each other.

❑ We spend quality time together.

❑ We trust each other.

❑ We choose to love each other.

❑ We have consistent rules and realistic godly expectations.

❑ We respect each other's privacy and individual worth.

❑ Our home is a loving, warm environment.

❑ Effective and open communication is encouraged.

❑ We use problem-solving techniques for complex issues and a plan for how such issues will be handled.

❑ We forgive each other.

❑ We have established relationships with other blended families or a spiritual support group.

Communication can be verbal or nonverbal. Communication is also listening and responding. Speaking is very powerful.

Effective communication is very valuable in developing lasting relationships. Communication is the process by which information is transmitted and exchanged. It is the exchanging of ideas verbally, non-verbally, or in writing. Effective communication takes place when the message conveyed is sent by the sender and received and acknowledged by the recipient. Communication is also listening and tone of voice. Communication can be positive, negative, informative, confusing, or conflicting. The sender can check on how the message was interpreted by the recipient by asking for feedback.

Effective verbal communication is a method of communication that is very important to developing a strong marital and parent-child bond. Speaking is a method of communication that can be either encouraging or discouraging, or it can build up or tear down an individual. Believers are cautioned by Scripture to control the tongue and speak words of kindness (Eph. 4:29, 32). Have you ever noticed that some people are very tactful and careful with words when speaking to acquaintances, but they may have a difficult time speaking tactfully towards their spouse, children, and other family members? Christians must speak the truth in love, control angry words, speak words of encouragement and healing, avoid unkind or bitter speech, and speak words of forgiveness. Words can be used like a sharp sword (Isa. 49:2) or they can communicate with a gentle spirit (1 Thess. 2:7).

A soft answer turns away wrath, but a harsh word stirs up anger. The tongue of the wise uses knowledge rightly, but the mouth of fools pours forth foolishness (Prov. 15:1–2).

Let no corrupt communication proceed out of your mouth, but what is good for necessary edification, that it may impart grace to the hearers (Eph. 4:29).

Effective communication cultivates assertiveness, closeness, shared experiences, bonding, warmth and affection, openness, and honesty.

When we communicate directly, we are being assertive. One way to ensure directness is to make "I" statements. An "I" statement involves three parts. It begins with the I and then describes what the person is feeling and what the other person is doing or not doing to contribute to that feeling. An additional part of the "I" message is a specific statement of what you would like. For example, a stepparent may say to a stepchild, "I feel hurt when you come home from school and don't say hello. I would like you to say hello when you come through the door." "I" messages encourage people to take responsibility for their feelings. Commonly used "You" messages often put people on the defensive and create barriers to communication. The "You" message says something about the other person and tends to be judgmental. For example, "Why don't you say hello when you come home from school?" I messages encourage more open, direct communication.[6]

Communication is an important factor in determining the types of relationships a person forms with others. It is very important in blended families for communication to be as open and as honest as possible. Families must trust one another in an effort to dispel those fears of communication. Feelings and thoughts must be directly communicated without fear of reprisal or discipline. If persons within the family are unable to communicate their feelings openly and honestly, relationships may deteriorate.

Allow others to share emotions, including crying. Say to the person, "We are going to get through this together." Don't retreat, isolate, or withdraw from the individual because they are upset. This is very important in the marriage relationship. Husbands and wives have a tendency to retreat and not be sensitive to the other spouse's emotional concerns. Retreating or withdrawing breaks the oneness. Your spouse is the person that should meet your emotional needs. Many people have sought other individuals to fulfill this void. This begins with communicating to another individual the hurt that you may be experiencing, only to find that they are caught up in an affair that they are having a difficult time severing. This emotional attachment is very dangerous and should only be reserved for your spouse. Couples must not compromise their integrity or morals to gain intimacy. This vulnerable time must be shared with your spouse to promote closeness and intimacy in your relationship.

Intimacy involves closeness, caring, shared experiences, bonding, warmth, affection, openness, and honesty. Intimacy is important in a marriage relationship. Remain committed to your spouse, be transparent, open and admit weaknesses, shortcomings and struggles. Trust one another and get to know one another. Intimacy grows when couples risk greater openness; couples learn to be emotionally present with each other. When couples develop a high degree of caring for each other a climate of trust is based on commitment to fidelity and continuity.[7]

For this reason a man will leave his father and mother and be united to his wife, and they will become one flesh (Gen. 2:24).

Barriers To Communication

(Place an (X) next to area(s) where you need improvement)

- ☐ Unresolved anger.
- ☐ Selective perception. Listening to only part of the message being conveyed.
- ☐ Unresolved fears.
- ☐ Extraneous distractions.
- ☐ Information overload.
- ☐ Not knowing how or when to communicate message.
- ☐ Failure to understand message.
- ☐ Lack of interest in message, tendency to tune out.
- ☐ Nonverbal messages conveying disinterest to sender.

- ☐ Sharp tongue, put downs, threats, character attacks, shouting, etc.
- ☐ Refusal to consider another opinion due to personal opinion.
- ☐ Frequent negative messages.
- ☐ Tuning out and not responding.
- ☐ Lack of understanding that women are emotional.
- ☐ Lack of understanding that men are logical.
- ☐ Poor timing. You communicate at times when the receiver may not be interested in talking on the subject
- ☐ Disrespectful tone of voice.

Husbands and wives should feel free to communicate honestly. Every problem should be talked through. Opportunities for talking should be valued. When communicating, remember to think before you speak. This rule should be used when you communicate to anyone—not just your spouse. Communicating using words such as honey, baby, or sweetheart before you make a statement smoothes over what might have been interpreted as a harsh statement. If you feel your mate is not communicating, tell him or her of your need to communicate. When communicating about issues, do not rehash old conversations; you will likely hear, "I don't remember saying that."

In other relationships, you are to "Be kindly affectionate to one another with brotherly love, in honor giving preference to one another" (Rom. 12:10).

Communication barriers interfere with the flow of communication. Any number of factors can interfere with messages in the process of communicating.

Handling Conflict

But avoid foolish and ignorant disputes, knowing that they generate strife. And a servant of the Lord must not quarrel but be gentle to all, able to teach, patient, in humility correcting those who are in opposition, if God perhaps will grant them repentance, so that they may know the truth, and that they may come to their senses and escape the snare of the devil, having been taken captive by him to do his will (2 Tim. 2:23–26).

Disagreements are very common and are inevitable in all relationships. We are in these relationships so that we can honor God and so that we can manifest His love for us to the world. It is not humanly possible to live in total harmony at all times; however, we are called to work towards peace.

Blessed are the peacemakers for they shall be called sons of God (Matt. 5:9).

Believers must learn to manage conflict in their lives. Conflict must not trigger violent behavior, angry outbursts,

58

Handling Conflict

Key Points to Remember When Handling Conflict

Pray about the situation, issue, or problem. Pray together or individually.

Determine what the issue is. Face and confront the problem. Get to the REAL issue. Go immediately to the person to talk about the issue.

Moreover, if your brother sins against you, go and tell him his fault between you and him alone. If he hears you, you have gained your brother (Matt. 18:15).

Treat the person with respect when the person is expressing feelings. Remember their opinion is theirs. God made us different and unique.

Listen very carefully to the person's feelings. Let the person tell his or her side. Allow the person speaking to talk without interrupting, being defensive, or discrediting their opinion.

Therefore, my beloved brethren, let every man be swift to hear, slow to speak, slow to wrath (James 1:19).

Talk about solutions and alternatives. Discuss the possible impact of solutions. Write them down if necessary.

Sometimes listing solutions on paper and talking through issues will help people to focus on the real problems and their solutions. It also reduces the possibility of getting sidetracked.

Weigh the pros and cons of solutions. Be open to trying a solution. Be prayerful when making a decision.

Talk with humility. Don't have an "I'm going to win this" mentality.

Don't criticize the other person's perspective. Criticism is used to diffuse the issue and to deflect attention away from the faults of the person who is criticizing.

Don't avoid conflict and pretend it does not exist or give in just to keep the peace.

Don't try to settle conflicts when you are angry. Request to talk later. Go for a walk or exercise to calm or cool down. Doing something to cool down allows you to clear your head.

Stop in the midst of your conflict and pray to God for direction in resolving this situation. The Holy Spirit will provide guidance.

Agree on a solution.

Forgive the person and move on to peace. Replace bitterness with gentleness. Don't hold grudges and constantly remind the person of the problem.

Not all conflict can be easily resolved. We must understand that conflict is often God's way of teaching us a valuable lesson we need to learn in order to continue to mature in our walk with Christ. Count it all as joy because it is a test of faith.

---

or isolation, but it must be handled in a loving way. If conflict is not managed properly, it can harm relationships.

Conflict in families must be handled and settled immediately. "Agree with your adversary quickly . . . " (Matt. 5:25). If the conflict is not resolved, it can build to resentment and eventually an explosive situation. Families must communicate honestly, gently, and with love. "Speak the truth in love"

(Eph. 4:15). Persons involved in a conflicting situation must be humble and considerate when resolving conflicts.

In blended families conflict is expected because of the different beliefs, experiences, and values each family member experiences and brings into the household.

It is our human nature to feel that we are correct in our opinion about how things should be. We have a tendency to become selfish and defensive when handling conflict. There are many immediate families and extended family members that refuse to speak to each other or be in the company of each other because of unresolved conflict.

Believers must work towards not causing discord by discussing openly any issue of concern, forgiving, and moving beyond the conflict towards reconciliation.

Now I urge you, brethren, note those who cause divisions and offenses, contrary to the doctrine which you learned, and avoid them (Rom. 16:17).

My brethren, count it all joy when you fall into various trials (James 1:2).

Professional Christian counseling should be sought if families are unable to handle conflict. God's Word, in Matthew 18:14-18 instructs us to seek counsel when we are unable to resolve conflict between us.

Family Meetings

"And Jacob called his sons and said, 'Gather together, that I may tell you what shall befall you in the last days: Gather together and hear, you sons of Jacob, and listen to Israel your father'" (Gen. 49: 1–2).

Arrange family meetings on a day when everyone can participate. The purpose of the meeting is to discuss issues and goals. Too often we only have discussions with our children when something adverse has occurred. These are generally difficult attempts to communicate at best. It is far easier to talk to your children when they and you are not stressed out.

Family Meetings

Guidelines for Family Meetings:
1. Allow enough time for the meeting.
2. Allow each person to speak without interruption.
3. Show each person respect for their individual opinions.
4. If necessary, take notes so that each person can remember what was discussed.
5. Allow everyone to have input into solutions.
6. Promote communicating with love.
7. Use this time effectively. Suggestions may need to be incorporated into the working agreement.

Family Worship

The home must provide a vital example of true Christianity. Children must be taught to talk to God about everything. (Matt 18:19, 20) Faith must become part of everyday life. We must make Bible reading and prayer a routine. Family worship can be incorporated into the family meeting time, or it can be separate. This is also a great time to open the channels of communications.

Family worship is an ideal time not only to offer up prayers to God and give thanks for all the blessings He has given you, but it is a warm and loving time where family members can openly share feelings. You will find that after praising God and confessing your sins to Him, you are more willing to open up to discussing issues that affect children that you may have been uncomfortable discussing in the past, such as girlfriends, boyfriends, friends, teachers, school, and any other issues of concern.

Family worship provides a non-threatening environment for open and candid discussion. You will be surprised at how much your children will share with you when you listen with respect. You must always remember to end these discussions in prayer. In doing this, it will allow your children to hear you humble yourself to God and ask for forgiveness of all the wrong things you may have done. Praying with your children also teaches them to seek guidance from God in every situation they encounter. A warm trusting fellowship with each other may take time to develop, but it is surely worth the effort.

The Roles of Stepparents

And he lifted his eyes and saw the women and children, and said, "Who are these with you?" And he said, "The children whom God has graciously given your servant" (Gen. 33:5).

God has allowed you to raise His children. Being a parent involves much more than fulfilling a biological function. Whether you are a stepparent or biological parent, God has assigned you the task of loving, raising, training, and developing the character of His children. "And that from childhood you have known the Holy Scriptures, which are able to make you wise for salvation through faith which is in Christ Jesus" (2 Tim. 3:15).

Parents must believe that children are a gift from God and that parenting is an awesome godly task that must be taken seriously. "Parents should not see children as simply a by-product of a biological function and miss completely the divine significance attached to parenthood. Children are a heritage from the Lord and the fruit of the womb is a reward. They are to us what God makes them, comforts or crosses. They are blessings not burdens. God says that these are my children which you have born unto me."[8]

When attempting to fulfill this awesome task the new blended family has created, the stepparent's role may not be clearly defined.

The Unexpected Role Conflict

The word stepparent is defined as "the person who has married one's parent after death or divorce from another parent."[9] Stepparents often enter marriage with undefined roles. They don't realize that there is a need for role definition until after the marriage. Stepmothers often enter the marriage with visions of healing a broken family through love and understanding. Jane Hurwiz, author of "Coping in a Blended Family," indicates that

Stepmothers tend to blend more easily if her natural children live with her. If a stepmother's biological children live elsewhere, the mother may feel guilty raising stepchildren when she cannot raise her own. Her attitude helps with the transition. A stepmother who behaves as a concerned adult or as an additional parent will have the least amount of adjustment problems with her stepchildren. A stepmother who wants to be a replacement mother may discover that her stepchildren resent her and resist even her best intentions.[10]

Stepfathers may believe that their new children will welcome a disciplinarian who can bring order into their lives. Jane Hurwiz further states that,

Many believe it is easier to be a stepfather than a stepmother. There is less cultural pressure for men to nurture and care for children. It is more common for children to live with their stepfather and their biological mother on a continual basis, which provides a stage for possible bonding.

In addition, stepfathers face their own unique problems. Discipline and money are common problems. Another issue is that of injustice. Even the most sensitive stepfather will hear complaints of injustice from stepchildren if he assumes the role of disciplinarian. A power struggle between stepfather and stepchildren will occur whenever stepfathers try to assume a disciplinarian role too quickly. In response to the turmoil, many stepfathers give up on communicating with their stepchildren and disengage from the stepfather role. They rationalize, "I married the mother, not the children."[11]

Stepfathers have also complained about their inability to fulfill the "head of household" role that God intends to exist within the family structure. The father or head of household may feel that his wife has a responsibility separate from his that she shares with another man, the children's father. The stepfather may have a difficult time being the father he would like to be to the children whose natural father shows up on weekends to take them away for fun times and excitement. His leadership may be affected because of constant interference from his wife, who allows this to happen, and the absent parent who appears to be the "good guy" because there is no discipline by this parent. The wife may not want to burden the stepfather with the responsibilities of her biological children when they have an involved parent. This is a very sensitive situation.

The solution to this issue is to always follow court-ordered visitation agreements. It is suggested that an every-other-weekend policy be instituted, however, this may require revising the court order. Most courts will not allow a parent to have every weekend with a child. This arrangement would not allow the custodial parent to have leisure time with the child. Most parents spend weeknights helping children with homework, transporting them to and from activities, preparing dinner, and attempting to maintain the structured schedule of a busy household where both husband and wife work. The more suitable arrangement of every other weekend, would also allow time for the children to spend with the stepparents in a more leisurely environment, so they can develop the quality relationship with one another that is desired. The father's leadership and authority role must not be affected by the absent parent's involvement in the child's life. The stepfather can be, through prayer and the study of God's Word, the strength the family needs. The wife must release the protective spirit that she has and understand that through prayer and through her husband's godly leadership, "all things will work together for good to those who love God"(Rom. 8:28). Chapter 9 will address this issue further.

Unclear Judgments and Perceptions

Children may struggle with the new stepparent's authority and complain to their biological parent that they feel treated unfairly. In some cases, they are right, because it is hard—very hard—to treat another person's child with the same compassion and understanding as you would your own child. Or, the stepparent is sometimes more objective when it comes to the stepchild and therefore appears less understanding and even critical. Thus, in an attempt to really demonstrate their own good parenting and genuine caring, the stepparent will make comments or judge behavior of the stepchild in a way that feels harsh to the child and promotes defensiveness in the biological parent. This is where that protective spirit comes out of a parent who feels his/her child is being mistreated. This is why it is so important for parents to raise children based on Biblical principles.

Parental Responsibilities

Children should be taught values that will help develop their character. Criticism of a child should be constructive. Pray for your children. Teach them what Jesus would do in any situation that they may encounter. Always watch the harsh tongue when talking to children. Never attack their character by calling them names, belittling them, and making them feel they don't measure up to your standards. They have to follow your guidance and God's standards. Children have a responsibility to obey their parents. Rules and expectations must be communicated to children, and they must follow them. Unfortunately, in a blended family it often takes years before children and parents adjust to these dramatic and unexpected changes that they continually face. If parenting styles differ drastically and an agreement cannot be reached, seek Christian counseling. Through prayer, communication, understanding, and trust, your parenting styles will be on one accord.

The Bible does not specifically address stepparenting, but we can assume from reading Bible stories that many related and unrelated people lived within one household. Parents cared for and, in some cases, adopted children who were not biologically related to the custodial parent(s).

Parents must pray that the Lord will provide them with the understanding, patience, and skills necessary to be a parent. It appears that we have become so conditioned to focus on our wants and needs and to acquire as much as we can, that we have completely forgotten about the basics of the family. In this society, we are taught through classroom instruction that will help us become effective and efficient employees, but we are not taught parenting skills. These skills are learned through trial and error, from parents, grandparents, or from others family members. Pray that God will develop your character to be the person you need to be to raise your children, and that He will provide guidance on how to handle your children effectively.

Then Manoah prayed to the Lord, and said, "O my Lord, please let the Man of God whom You sent come to us again and teach us what we shall do for the child who will be born" (Judg. 13:8).

Stepparents should learn from Joseph who was Jesus Christ's adopted father and stepparent. Although his circumstances were unique, he was considered the legal father of Jesus. Joseph showed qualities of humility and gentleness. Parents can learn from Joseph's four important qualities for godly parents and stepparents:

• "He always did what the Lord asked him to do (Matt. 1:24). Joseph was a good man and was merciful and obedient. He took Mary as his wife with no complaints or concerns. He was not disobedient to the heavenly vision.
• He allowed others to give good things to the child in his care. The wise men presented their gifts to Baby Jesus (Matt. 2:11).
• Joseph always acted quickly to protect his child (Matt. 2:14, 15).
• Joseph trained Jesus in his trade as a carpenter."[12]

Joseph exemplified the type of relationship stepparents should have with their stepchildren. Stepparents

(Step)Parents Must Recognize:

Place an (X) next to the areas that you and your spouse must change.

- ❑ That prayer, patience, love, wisdom, and commitment are the key ingredients to the success of a (blended) family.
- ❑ That a blended family working agreement is necessary.
- ❑ That the stepfamily is different from the traditional family.
- ❑ That the children you are caring for are God's children.
- ❑ That the parent-child relationship preceded the new couple's relationship.
- ❑ That stepparents cannot replace the natural parent(s) no matter how terrible the natural parent may seem. Divided loyalties also exist that often make it difficult for children to relate to all parental adults in their lives.
- ❑ That it is not necessary to come on too strong. Loving and building a relationship takes time. The relationships must be developed. If the stepparent is patient and loving, most children will develop feelings of attachment and caring.
- ❑ That unrealistic/untrue fairy tale myths about the mean, wicked stepparent exists in this society.
- ❑ That stepchildren may be resistant to stepparent authority and may complain to the biological parent that they are not treated fairly.

- ❑ That they must work very hard to promote unity within the family and harmony and peace in the home.
- ❑ That open and honest communication is very important.
- ❑ That building a cooperative relationship with the absent parent and grandparents is important.
- ❑ That children will have natural feelings for their biological parents. Do not take this personally. The child probably feels the same about the stepparent.
- ❑ That a certain level of confusion exists for the children. Expect ambivalent feelings of love and dislike initially.
- ❑ That visiting children must live by the rules in the home. You can't be "Santa Claus" or the "buddy" because you don't see your kids often. When you discipline, you are providing godly guidance for your children.
- ❑ That you cannot expect instant love, but you should provide unconditional love towards each other.
- ❑ That the stepfather is the head of his household. He guides, supports, disciplines, and listens to the children.

have more influence on the children in the household than a biological parent who does not live with the child on a day to day basis. Therefore, stepparents must pray that they set a godly example for their children. They must also pray that they gain patience, tolerance, fortitude, courage, grace, and wisdom so that they might impart it to their children, even when the children

may be reluctant to receive it.

Stepparents must allow the child's affection for the absent parent to flourish by being respectful of the relationship the child has with the absent parent. Adults must accept the fact that children can show affection to more than two parental adults. Adults should avoid competing for a child's affection and should encourage the child to enjoy a positive relationship with the biological parent and stepparent. If the parent is deceased, allow the child to grieve and express feelings about the deceased parent.

Issues Parents Should Discuss Before the Marriage

There are additional issues parents must discuss before the marriage.

• Values, traditions, and morals relative to child rearing.
• The amount of time the couple will spend with children during the courtship.

It is recommended that couples seek Christian premarital counseling and develop a blended family working agreement before the marriage.

DISCIPLINE

My son, do not despise the Lord's discipline and do not resent his rebuke, because the Lord disciplines those he loves, as a father the son he delights in (Prov. 3:11, 12 NIV).

"Why do they act like this! Mine have never acted like your kids!" Or, "You are too lenient on your kids, but you are hard on my kids." These are common statements in stepfamilies.

In some families parents have a difficult time with discipline because of guilt, fears, or past experiences. Discipline is necessary for the stability of the children. Discipline shapes and molds the character in children.

In blended families, confusion over disciplinary roles and distorted perceptions contribute to marital conflict and resentment in children. According to Emily and John Visher, founders of the Stepfamily Association of America and recognized researchers in the area of stepfamilies, "Even though there is marital satisfaction, research is indicating that often stepfamilies do not stay together when positive stepparent/stepchild relationships are not developed. Dynamically, this is quite different from first marriages."[13] Conflict over rules, discipline, and authority are consequences of remarriage, especially when there is a conflict with past family traditions and beliefs regarding discipline.

Disciplining a stepchild can be uncomfortable in many families. Even the most sensitive stepparent will hear complaints of injustice from stepchildren if the stepparent disciplines the child. This is because the stepchildren do not consider the stepparent a legitimate authority figure.

Good parents discipline their children. Parents must discipline and teach their children in order to prepare them for the future. This does not give parents a license for cruel or inhumane treatment. Parents are called to discipline, guide, and nurture children. Parents must teach children the skills of respect for authority, self control, consideration of others, and submission to God. The disastrous consequences of parental indulgence are dramatically illustrated in the lives of three of God's great servants; Eli, Samuel, and David. Eli's sin caused God to condemn his house forever. Eli did not raise and teach his sons in the ways of the Lord. They were vile and corrupt, and Eli did not restrain them. After Eli heard everything his sons were doing, he tried to correct them. Since Eli waited too long to correct his sons, they would not listen to him (1 Sam. 2).

Another example is the story of Samuel's sons. Israel rebelled against God because Samuel's sons who were their judges in Beersheba did not follow in their father's footsteps. They were intent on using dishonesty to gain their own profit by taking bribes and perverting the course of justice.

Abijah, David's son, rebelled and attempted to usurp King David's throne. At this time David was very old. David never corrected his son or questioned him. With conflict as a result of treason in a priestly dynasty and family, Israel's rejection of God was the result of the failure of some of God's greatest servants to discipline their children. It seems incredible that men so close to God would be careless in the discipline of their children (1 Sam. 8:3–5).

Today, parents are bombarded with worldly advice on how to raise children from doctors, psychologists, government, other parents, and others who leave the impression that we know absolutely nothing about rearing our own children. They are correct. Parents are not trained to be parents. Recently, an effort has been made to encourage parents to take formalized training classes. Christian parents can be comforted to know that the Bible provides a wealth of knowledge on how to raise children. Parents must pray that God will give them the guidance to raise children. Parents can be influenced by worldly views on how children should be raised. However, parents must not relinquish their God-given responsibility to guide children on the straight and narrow course of life. The way to teach a child is by example. God gave a high compliment to Abraham when he said, "For I have known him, in order that he may command his children and his household after him, that they keep the way of the Lord" (Gen. 18:19).

"The rod and reproof give wisdom, but a child left to himself brings shame to his mother. . . . Correct your son, and he will give you rest; yes, he will give delight to your soul" (Prov. 29:15–17).

A child who lives without parental discipline is doubly cheated. First, he is being taught to be self-centered. Secondly, he is subconsciously learning that his parents are not genuinely concerned about him. Parents who really love their children provide the necessary

Enhancing The Child's Development

Stepparents Can Contribute to the Child's Development By:

Receiving their children from God (Gen. 33:5; 1 Sam. 1:27).

Imparting godly knowledge, wisdom, and guidance (Prov. 22:6; Eph. 6:4).

Providing for the child's spiritual, physical, and emotional needs.

Being very in tune with their children.

Loving them unconditionally. Giving them frequent reassurance that they are loved (Titus 2:4).

Promoting open, honest communication among family members at all times. Family meetings are important.

Correcting children (Prov. 13:24).

(Mothers) *Nurturing* and being a mentor to their children.

(Fathers) *Demonstrating* a godly character in humility, tenderness, and patience.

Promoting a cordial relationship with absent parents and relatives.

Not arguing in front of children.

Allowing the children to spend time alone with each biological parent.

Attending school events, games, and other activities.

Helping them deal with anger, jealousy, rejection, depression, and guilt feelings they may experience. These feelings are normal. You may need to seek outside help.

Working out a viable financial plan and budget that is in the best interest of all family members.

Following all court-ordered agreements. Children need predictability and it supports stability in the home.

Obtaining court-ordered child support from absent parent, if possible (1 Tim. 5:8).

Not criticizing former spouse in front of the children. This will make a child feel protective towards the absent parent and will promote insecure feelings in the child. Always remember to be truthful if the child asks a question.

Allowing the stepchild the freedom to talk about the absent parent. This reduces loyalty conflicts.

Being a positive role model for the children. Do not set a bad example (Ezek. 20:18).

Not showing favoritism (Gen. 25:28; 33:2).

Not promoting resentment from the child by allowing the stepparent to assume the role of the authoritative parent early in the marriage. Instruction and discipline should be gradual and godly.

Setting rules in the home and enforcing them. Set limits.

Protecting them from evil.

Being consistent.

Allowing their relationship with stepchildren to grow with time. Don't jump in too fast and don't feel the need to compete with the biological parent.

Allowing the child, especially adult children, to decide how much mothering they need from a stepmom.

Not being sensitive when the children share their past experiences in the home. Encourage them to talk about their past experiences. Talking through these issues encourages the emotional bond between the child and the stepparent.

Spending time with biological parent to maintain closeness.

Setting clear limits on dress, nudity, and privacy in the home for everyone—especially when there are teenagers or young adults in the home.

Treating biological children and stepchildren equally. There should not be different standards. Responsibilities, rewards, and rules should be given equally (sometimes based on the age of the children).

Steps To Disciplining in a Stepfamily

Both the biological parent and stepparent must discipline children based on godly principles. There should be a balance of love and discipline. Discipline should never be harsh (Prov. 3:11–12, Eph. 6:4).

The couple must develop a written agreement on discipline of children—even visiting children.

Set up a discipline chart. The chart should tie rules to consequences. For example, if a child does not complete daily chores, he or she cannot play outside until the chores are completed. As the family blends and grows together, the discipline chart may not be needed.

Establish time frames and also rewards. All family members know what is expected and they also know what the consequences will be if rules are broken and what the rewards will be if rules are followed.

Establish boundaries based on the ages of children.

Parents must never interfere with the biological or stepparent's disciplining of a child. This will eliminate the child playing one parent against the other.

Avoid the "dominating dictatorial authority figure role." A stepparent who assumes too much authority too soon will cause loyalty conflicts for the children.

Balance rewards, punishment, love, and encouragement (Jer. 31:20). Parents must discipline with love. Do not be too lenient or too harsh. Differentiate between whether a child is being rebellious or simply ignorant of the offense.

Discipline should be perceived as positive (Prov. 22:15, Lam. 3:27).

Be consistent and don't vacillate. Always follow through. Don't let your personal feelings of fear and guilt get in the way of consistency.

Find ways to build your child's self esteem.

"The rod and reproof give wisdom, but a child left to himself brings shame to his mother" (Prov. 29:15). Child abuse is a concern in this world today. Spanking children should be the last resort after all else has failed (withdrawing privileges, etc.) Spanking must be gentle. If bruises or marks are visible, it is abuse.

Never discipline when you are angry. Keep a cool head (Ps. 6:1).

---

discipline to cause them to grow into well-adjusted adult life.

It is essential for a child to know that his parents care about his behavior, and that the way he thinks and acts really matters to them. God shows love for his children by disciplining them. The Bible says, "Whom the Lord loves He corrects; just as a father the son in whom he delights" (Prov. 3:12). If parents correct children with love, our children will sense that discipline implies love.

Parents who ignore their child's misbehavior will receive disrespect in return, resulting in further patterns of misbehavior. Repeated neglect of disciplinary action will have tragic lifetime consequences (Prov. 29:15–17).

Training of children is not primarily the responsibility of the psychologist, the church, or the school. It is the primary responsibility of parents (Eph. 6:4). We render a doubtful service to God and mankind, if we save the whole world yet lose our own children. God will help us make them what He would have them be.

Establishing boundaries is very important because children will know what is expected. Parents must discuss what the boundaries should be. There will be disagreements on what the boundaries should be. We encourage parents to have an open discussion in a calm environment and to be non-confrontational when discussing boundaries. Establish what the rules will be. Determine what you both can live with. If the two parents cannot agree, start with what you can agree on and work towards agreement in the other areas. Research what the rules should be, and if you are not sure, talk to others who have been very successful at raising children. You must remember you can not discipline a child for behavior that breaks boundaries that had not been clearly established and communicated to the child. Most of all, be consistent in your application of discipline. Children will watch to see if what you say is actually what you do. You will need to modify your boundaries and discipline as the children grow older and become more responsible. This will require some work on your part if you have several children of varying ages. But be sure to communicate with all the children the boundaries that are set for each based upon their respective ages and reassure the younger children that when they reach that age they will have the same boundaries.

You are God's child, and He loves you with an infinite and unconditional love. He has disciplined you, taught you, and encouraged you. He has asked that you pass these attributes on to your children. Parenting involves consistency, encouragement, communication, tolerance, and respect.

Parents in blended families must take the responsibility of parenting very seriously. It is an awesome task in this unique situation because of the challenges that these families face.

Stepfathers and stepmothers, be united in all you do in seeking the peace and harmony you desire for your blended family.

Family Traditions

Behold, how good and how pleasant it is for brethren to dwell together in unity!— Psalm 133:1

A key solution for helping the blended family grow together is to establish family traditions that are different from those previously experienced. Developing traditions provides meaning for family interactions and it gives each member of the family an event to look forward to and remember always. "A family tradition is the passing on of knowledge, practices, and customs from one generation to the next. Even those who claim to be against traditions are influenced by them. Traditions are developed by repeating rituals that help us remember an important event. As we pass on the tradition, we also continue to relive the initial event." Establishing traditions helps a family become unified and stable. Traditions give people a sense of belonging and connection to those who have gone on before them and those who will come after them. It is one way to help give blended families a sense of longevity and stability.[14]

[A tradition] reminds our children to remember. It says, "pay attention, this is important." The challenge for parents is to create significant traditions rather than meaningless ones. This is crucial to blended families because they come together with joint histories. Traditions that integrate the past, present, and future can be part of stepfamily integration.[15]

A key ingredient that unites and maintains traditional families is the sharing of family histories from one generation to another. This can be difficult for blended families because there is no commonality initially when the family members move in together. Establishing traditions in a blended family is a critical element to its success.

An effective method of initially developing the relationship between the stepparent and the stepchildren is for the stepparent to discuss his or her family history. The children should know the stepparents' family history. A discussion of childhood memories, funny stories, or experiences helps form the bond between the stepparent and the stepchildren. Share childhood pictures. The children might be surprised at how much they have in common with the stepparent. Sharing this information will also help the bond between stepchildren and extended family members.

Allow the children to share memories. Children are sometimes afraid to share their past experiences with new family members. Stepparents and biological parents may be uncomfortable with children sharing this information. Children must be allowed to be as open as possible about their experiences. The family may consider incorporating some of these experiences into new family traditions.

Holiday traditions can sometimes be very difficult to establish because children may spend time with their other parent on alternate holidays. Think of something unique all of you can do together like buying a Christmas tree and decorating it two or three weeks before Christmas. Or a new tradition could be that each member of the family buys or makes an ornament that symbolizes a happy time within the family to put on the tree.

It is important for the family to create scrapbooks, videotapes, audiotapes, and/or photo albums of the new blended family of memorable events. Take pictures at special events or family trips. Make note cards on a funny thing that happened on that day.

Edward and I established various family traditions that we all look forward to. We have family night or fun night at least once a week. Looking forward to "family night" helps to bring us all together regularly for a long period of time. We rent a family video, order pizza, snacks, and all the good stuff kids like to eat and watch movies or play games. The kids look forward to this. We also have our family Super Bowl party. My daughters and I look forward to shopping together and attending ballet and tap dance classes together in addition to many other activities. Edward and the boys will go to the driving range to hit golf balls, watch sports on television, and cook a special dinner for the girls. Every year, Edward will take the girls to a Father-Daughter banquet at church. This is an event they all look forward to.

God used traditions as a way of allowing us to remember events but also as a way of helping us find direction. Abraham's descendants discussed the stories of their family for many generations because they heard God speaking in and through those events, not only in the past but also in the present situations they faced.

Establishing an Agreement

"Can two walk together, unless they are agreed?" Amos 3:3

Establishing a written agreement is crucial in helping the blended family work through complex issues. It also helps to promote consistency when emotions get in the way of making decisions that are in the family's best interest. You may feel this is not necessary; however, an agreement will minimize conflicts, and it can be referred to and revised when needed. This agreement can be discussed and written prior to the marriage or at any time during the relationship.

A couple may want to write out as a separate agreement their pledge to each other. It may include the statement that you promise to love, honor, and cherish each other. You may state that you will continue to study your roles as husband/wife, and that you will not break the marriage covenant.

The Bible speaks to the issue of establishing a written agreement to eliminate confusion and distress. In the verse below, the purpose of the agreement was to help restrain the Israelites from making the wrong decision that may have caused them to sin again.

And because of all this, we make a sure covenant and write it (Neh. 9:38).

"This agreement was necessary because of the Israelites' frequent departure from God. They decided to make a firm (sure) written covenant with Him. It was sealed and made part of the record. They were in agreement when they made it, and it was done unanimously, that they might strengthen the hands of one another. It was sealed by priests, Levites, and priests on behalf of others."[16]

Establishing an agreement forces the couple to communicate and work through issues. An agreement will promote peace, harmony, and unity in the home.

Now I plead with you brethren, by the name of our Lord Jesus Christ, that you all speak the same thing, and that there be no divisions among you, but that you be perfectly joined together in the same mind and in the same judgment (1 Cor. 1:10).

Discuss openly and candidly with your spouse the need to clearly define the roles of both parents with each child and the role of the outside parent, siblings, and other relatives. Existing agreements such as visitation agreements must be included in the new agreement. Keep in mind that a court-ordered visitation agreement must not be modified unless all parties agree, and a new agreement is issued by the court. The court-ordered agreement must be followed to promote consistency in the children's lives. The ideal situation is when all parties can unanimously and cordially work together in the best interest of everyone involved.

CONTENTMENT

"Godliness with contentment is great gain."—1 Timothy 6:6

Contentment means being satisfied with what God has given you.

For a day in Your courts is better than a thousand. I would rather be a doorkeeper in the house of my God than dwell in the tents of wickedness. For the Lord God is a sun and shield; the Lord will give grace and glory; no good thing will He withhold from those who walk uprightly (Ps. 84:10–12).

Contentment is accepting the past and rejoicing in this day the Lord has made.

This is the day the Lord has made; we will rejoice and be glad in it (Ps. 118:24).

Contentment is a choice and a quality that promotes happiness. Happiness is enjoying everything the Lord has given you.

Happiness is a feeling of spiritual contentment that will carry you through the trials and heartaches of

Establishing An Agreement

Decide what should be included in the agreement.
The following are a few suggestions:

1. Description of husband's and wife's biblical parental roles in the home.
2. Information contained in visitation agreements and other court agreements.
3. Establish couple time together (vacation without children), as well as other times away from children.
4. Agreement on family quality time together.
5. Plan in advance for holidays/parental visitation so that children know what is expected.
6. Parameters relative to outside influences, particularly with ex-partners.
7. Child-rearing values.
8. Agreements on what children will call the stepparent.
9. Financial issues such as establishing an annual spending plan or savings plan to pay for children's expenses such as college, outside activities, clothes, toys, summer camp, health care expenses, etc.
10. Expectations of visiting children, and children living in the home. (Chores, bedtimes, school work, etc.) Adolescent, young adult, and adult children must be included in the agreement.
11. What role each parent will play in disciplining the children. If parents are in disagreement in the area of discipline, seek professional help. Parents must be in agreement.
12. Rules of the home.
13. Family worship.
14. Family meeting. Use this time to make changes to the agreement, if necessary.
15. Establish a time that the biological parent can be alone with the child or children, to help maintain the relationship and to help overcome the loss.
16. Include the stepparent's quality time with stepchildren to help develop the relationship. For example, doing a school project together, going out to the movies, or doing special activities of interest to the stepchild.
17. Establish ideas for new family traditions. Remember to include past family traditions. Get ideas from the children.
18. Indicate how tasks and household responsibilities will be shared in the family. Responsibilities must be based on age.
19. Discuss setting aside a private area for visiting children so that they feel part of the family home. Agree on where this should be. You may want to designate an empty drawer that will remain empty until the child visits.
20. Agree on what will be kept at the home for visiting children. (Toys, clothes, etc.)
21. Discuss how to minimize the attraction visiting adolescents or young adult children may have for another adolescent or young adult child who lives in the family home.

This agreement should be formalized based on your unique situations. It should be discussed and updated periodically as circumstances change.

life with calm stability and peace of mind. Happiness is also an act of the will. Things will happen in your life that you have no control over that will give you a reason to be unhappy. We have the power through Christ to make our own response to those happenings. Happiness is a choice. Happiness is enjoying everything the Lord has given you and not fretting about the things that have been taken away or withheld.

Contentment does not mean a state of stagnation. Seek God through prayer to change circumstances in your life. Trust that God will give you all you need. It is very difficult to feel a state of contentment when some needs have not been met. How is it possible for a person to achieve contentment? In this world we tend to seek contentment from external sources. We measure our happiness and joy by worldly standards. God said He will provide all our needs if we believe and trust in Him. Desire not the things of this world but rejoice in where you are.

Spiritual contentment comes only from within, it is not from things of this world. You cannot buy it or work for it, nor can it be given to you. It only comes from the belief in Christ Jesus, and it cannot be taken away by this world no matter what people go through in life.

You can be content with little!

A little that a righteous man has is better than the riches of many wicked. For the arms of the wicked shall be broken, but the Lord upholds the righteous (Ps. 37:16–17).

Be grateful for what you have. Be content with your spouse, family, children, job, past, and everything else, and accept God's plan for your future. Live within your income.

"It is good to give thanks to the Lord . . . "(Ps. 92:1).

Likewise the soldiers asked him, saying, "And what shall we do?" So he said to them, "Do not intimidate anyone or accuse falsely, and be content with your wages" (Luke 3:14).

Finally, enjoy your life!

So I commended enjoyment, because a man has nothing better under the sun than to eat, drink, and be merry; for this will remain with him in his labor for the days of his life which God gives him under the sun (Eccl. 8:15).

Chapter 9

Outside Influences

But avoid foolish and ignorant disputes,
knowing that they generate strife. And a
servant of the Lord must not quarrel but be
gentle to all, able to teach, patient . . .
                    —2 Timothy 2:23–24

Cordial relationships with former partners are encouraged. We applaud those who are able to work cooperatively with former partners and relatives.

However, custody arrangements can become a new battleground for the power struggle that took place during the previous marriage. Children are being used in a constant tug-of-war. Former spouses must work towards peace with each other. The family home must be free from negative outside influences that may impede the gelling of family relationships and the growth and development of the children within the new family unit. These outside influences should encourage and not hinder growth and development. It is important that parents in the family home manage their relationships with former spouses, partners, and others who may have an influence on the family. The ideal situation is one in which everyone can work together to promote peace and harmony. Any influence on the children should be positive and should contribute to the development of godly character in the children. Cordial relationships are important and are in the best interest of children.

Former partners are sometimes filled with bitterness, which makes working together cooperatively extremely difficult. Believers must be mindful of their attitude towards the opposition. Do not be quarrelsome but kindly. Matt. 5:38–48 states,

You have heard that it was said, "An eye for an eye and a tooth for a tooth." But I tell you not to resist an evil person. But whoever slaps you on your right cheek, turn the other to him also. If anyone wants to sue you and take away your tunic, let him have your cloak also. And whoever compels you to go one mile, go with him two. Give to him who asks you and from him who wants to borrow from you do not turn away. You have heard that it was said, you shall love your neighbor and hate your enemy. But

I say to your love your enemies, bless those who curse you, do good to those who hate you, and pray for those who spitefully use you and persecute you, that you may be sons of your Father in heaven for He makes His sun rise on the evil and on the good and sends rain on the just and on the unjust. For if you love those who love you, what reward have you? Do not even the tax collectors do the same? And if you greet your brethren only, what do you do more than others? Do not even the tax collectors do so? Therefore you shall be perfect, just as your Father in heaven is perfect.

Negative outside influences can cause serious problems in the marriage and affect relationships between step-parents, biological parents, and children. Children who want to be loyal to biological parents are often caught in the middle. Parents take advantage of this by expecting children to take sides in an effort to divide or diminish loyalty. When parents place children in this situation, they are not loving them but selfishly using them. Parents are encouraged to be understanding and to love their children unconditionally

Parents must put aside selfishness and think about what is in the children's best interest. It takes a great deal of forgiveness and acceptance to handle this situation. It is important for custodial parents and non-custodial parents to work together at providing children with the love and support of both birth parents. In some extreme situations, however, such as in the case when children are being abused, the contact must be limited or prohibited.

Hostile former non-custodial partners often feel rejected, as a result of the loss of children and, in some cases, the loss of partners. Some former partners have difficulty understanding the limitations on their involvement in the blended family. Former spouses who have not been able to accept their loss will sometimes intentionally interfere with the family.

Couples in blended families must be careful that outside influences do not undermine the leadership in their home. Parents should treat each other with respect for their children's benefit. In cases of joint custody, communication and cooperation is essential. Ground rules must be clearly established and followed. Parents must put aside their personal feelings and put the children's interests first. This is often very difficult for adults to do as a result of the feelings of brokenness, bitterness, and emotional and physical loss.

In spite of the closeness of the marriage, outside influences can contribute to the break up of a marriage. The couple must attempt to remove areas of contention by developing an agreement on how outside influences will be handled.

Consistency of visitation is important to the security of the children and it also establishes a consistent pattern for the absent parent. Coordinating schedules and routines of everyone involved can be stressful and a source of conflict. However, for both parents and children, visitation is critical to maintaining a sense of connectedness. Bitter spouses may find ways to spoil visitation such as not showing up to pick up a child. Children should be helped through a difficult transition by making visitation successful. Both parents must accept that their children have two homes—one with mom and one with dad. Visiting children should not be treated as guests—they are members of the household.

Tips on Handling Outside Influences

1. Establish parameters.
2. Allow children time with biological parents. Follow all court-ordered visitation agreements if they exist.
3. Promote cordial, courteous relationships with former spouses, partners, and former in-laws.
4. Treat former partners with respect.
5. Allow your child to maintain a close relationship with his or her non-custodial parent.
6. Keep in mind what is in the best interest of the children.
7. Open the door to a good relationship with former extended family members as they are usually not included in visitation agreements.
8. Do not criticize the absent parent.
9. Don't allow outside annoyances to upset the marriage.
10. Refrain from playing games with ex-partners.
11. Keep the topic of conversation with ex-partners only on issues relative to the children. Your family's personal business is your business.
12. Plan for holidays so that children are given time with each parent. This may not be possible if the biological parent lives out of the area.
13. Lower your expectation about holidays. You may not always be able to spend time with the children.
14. Discuss with former partner the need to establish similar rules in both homes. This will promote consistency with the children.
15. Encourage visitation that includes grandparents.
16. Do not respond to unreasonable demands of ex-spouses.
17. Do not become emotional with an ex-spouse. Keep conversations on a business level.
18. If it is unbearably difficult to talk to an ex-partner, allow a neutral party to act as a mediator to exchange information.
19. If it is impossible to communicate verbally, try written communication. E-mail or mailing a note to an ex-partner may be effective.
20. Promote direct contact between adults instead of sending messages through the children.
21. When children visit they must conform to the rules of the home. These rules must be communicated to them.
22. Establish rules regarding former spouses and their relatives.
23. Establish visitation agreements and keep commitments. If they must change, provide a written change. Use a calendar available for everyone.
24. Minimize calls to the family home (except in an emergency). Ex-partners should call each other at work if there is a need to discuss the children.
25. Ex-partners should call children at reasonable times, not just when it is convenient for them.
26. Visitation agreements must include specifics about summer vacations, holidays, special times, etc.
27. Ex-partners should be kept informed of special events. Mail special notices to the absent parent such as back-to-school night, sporting events, etc.
28. Spouses must agree on how to handle special events such as weddings of adult children, family reunions, and funerals when these events involve ex-spouses and relatives.
29. Allow children to buy gifts, etc., for the absent parent.

Whether children are visiting or leaving your home to visit a biological parent, visitation agreements must be in place and court orders must be honored, especially when dealing with uncooperative former partners.

In-laws and Relatives

In-laws in most families can have a positive influence on the marriage and family. In some families, however, meddlesome and antagonistic relatives as well as friends can interfere and negatively influence the marriage and family. The Bible states in Matt. 19:4–6:

He who made them at the beginning made them male and female, and for this cause shall a man leave his father and mother and shall cleave to his wife and the two shall become one flesh. So that they are no more two, but one flesh, what therefore God hath joined together, let not man put asunder.

Marriage is the closest relationship in life. Parents and other relatives must not interfere with the marriage and family relationships. This statement means the marriage should be free from the influence of parents and other relatives. This does not mean you are to cut off your relationship with in-laws and relatives.

Parents by nature love their children and want what is in their best interest. Children also love and admire their parents and respect their parents' opinions. Children usually establish the same or similar values and apply these values to their life, their marriage, and to raising their own children. But when people marry, they bring different values into the marriage. The couple should be allowed to work through the differences without the influence of relatives. The couple must be allowed to be independent and manage their own home as they see fit.

The couple's love and commitment for each other should be above the commitment to their parents and to extended family members. This does not mean you ignore, disrespect, mistreat, or abandon parents and relatives. The intimate relationship between parents and children should remain the same. Children must understand that parents also have years of experience and wisdom, and under certain circumstances may be able to assist children in resolving problems. This advice should only be given if children seek advice, and both the husband and wife must agree on going to parents to seek advice. Mark 7:10–13 states that children are to honor their parents. Children are obligated to take care of their parents when they are elderly and no longer able to care of themselves. Children are also required to take care of them financially if, for circumstances that are beyond the parents' control, they are not financially able to provide for themselves.

Grandparents must be honored as valuable family members. Grandparents provide a great deal of guidance and godly wisdom that can be passed on from generation to generation. Grandparents should be involved in helping to raise the children and in teaching them the Word of God.

In every situation, we are called to promote peace and harmony and to use biblical wisdom in handling even the most complex situation.

Chapter 10

Family Finances

So if you have not been trustworthy in handling worldly wealth, who will trust you with true riches?—Luke 16:11 NIV

Some common statements in blended families are: "He spent our money on his children and their mother, and he didn't ask me how I feel about this." "My stepmother pays for private school for her own children, but we have to go to public school." "She bought her child a car and paid for the other child's college tuition, and my children have to get a student loan for college."

You may say to yourself, "My power and the strength of my hands have produced this wealth for me." But remember the Lord your God, for it is He who gives you the ability to produce wealth, and so confirms His covenant, which He swore to your forefathers, as it is today (Deut. 8:17, 18 NIV).

Money is often a source of friction and is a sensitive and complex issue in blended families. There are serious financial pressures on a parent who is supporting two households. It is not unusual for the current wife to resent payments to the former wife.

A stepfather is the family member most often caught on all sides of the money problem. Since children usually live with their mothers after a divorce, fathers often pay child support to their former wives. A remarried father usually has his wife's children living with him as stepchildren, which adds to household expenses. Equal opportunity for all children is rarely achieved in any family, nuclear or not. Yet when blended families are involved, the idea of fairness is more elusive as the number of people involved increases. Children or spouses see this as favoritism.[1]

If we truly understand the purpose of money, then our burden becomes lighter. The purpose of money is not to free us from daily dependence on God, but to demonstrate God's love and power in our lives.

Starting over with children in the family can be expensive. Blended families must consider whether a larger home is needed to accommodate the additional children, or whether the couple plans to increase their family by having more children.

There is also conflict over the use of child support money. Should it be kept in a separate account to only be used for the children and not to be combined with the other family income? Should the money be placed in one resource?

Each of you must bring a gift in proportion to the way the Lord your God has blessed you (Deut. 16:17).

If anyone does not provide for his relatives, and especially for his immediate family, he has denied the faith and is worse than an unbeliever (1 Tim. 5:8 NIV).

Some families find there is never enough money, and sooner or later they squabble over it. When couples marry, they mesh different styles of handling money. This problem requires effective communication, time, and effort. If your money problems escalate, seek spiritual guidance. Realize that each of you will have different attitudes and values.

To one spouse, money may mean power. To the other, money may mean security or status. One may be a spender and the other a saver. The couple must communicate and compromise.

Good financial planning is part of wise stewardship. You must believe that your money is not yours but God's money. Having this perspective gives a person the freedom to use finances as a tool to accomplish God's purposes. We do not come into this world with possessions, and we will not leave with anything. Money is something that God uses to test your ability to handle the other gifts He desires to give you (Luke 16:11). God requires believers to avoid an overly consumptive lifestyle. Be moderate in all things (1 Cor. 9:25); avoid debt (Prov. 22:7; Rom. 13:8); maintain a savings program (Prov. 12:11); and set long-term goals (Prov. 13:22).

Evidences of Financial Bondage

Insecurity is the by-product of building our lives around persons, positions, or possessions which we know can be taken from us.

Fear occurs as we become aware of all of the possible ways in which we could lose our most cherished possessions.

Anxiety is the physical and emotional tension which results when we think about financial problems.

Loss of sleep: worry, and pressure from financial cares become greater at night and remove the possibility of peaceful sleep.

Ungratefulness: financial cares and concerns decrease our ability to appreciate or enjoy the many benefits God and others provide for us.

Enslavement: money and possessions have built-in demands for protection and maintenance. Thus, the things we own soon own us.

Envy is desiring to have what someone else has. It is the by-product of comparison. It robs us of the ability to enjoy what God has given to us.

Bitterness is the evidence that we love money and possessions more than we love God, because it is God who allows our possessions to be taken or destroyed so that He can build the character of Christ in our lives.

Disillusionment: when we attempt to use money to fulfill all our dreams, we discover that what we thought would make us happy and fulfilled only brings temporary pleasure and unforeseen disappointments.[2]

Poverty can be a result of following our natural inclinations. On the other hand, God's increase comes by developing a spirit of generosity according to God's direction.

Honor the Lord with your possessions, and with the firstfruits of all your increase: So your barns will be filled with plenty, and your vats will overflow (Prov. 3:9–10).

Financial issues are generally one of the most difficult areas to get a good handle on, and that is because they are filled with emotions. To be financially successful, both husband and wife must remove self from the money picture. They must seek God in every financial decision. Together they must become good stewards of God's possessions. The husband should have the final say over how money is to be spent, but not without the wise counsel of his wife. Remember, God holds the husband accountable for his house, wife, and family. They are a testimony to his walk with God.

God delights in having His children trust in Him for their daily needs. However, all too often when riches increase, it is easy to stop depending upon the Lord, and when we feel that we do not need the Lord, we lose our

love for Him. When this happens, God's remedy is to bring unexpected needs which force us to His Word and prayer. He then once again delights in giving us our daily needs, exceedingly and abundantly above all that we ask or think.

Husbands, listen to your wives. Many a financial disaster can be avoided by listening to your wife's cautions about a financial decision before it is made. God designed the wife to be "an help meet" for the husband (Gen. 2:18 KJV). As such, she has special abilities to sense dangers, which are often overlooked by her husband. "A wise man will hear, and increase learning . . . " (Prov. 1:5).

Solutions for Handling Finances

Generally, the husband handles the budget. However, if he does not wish to manage the money, his wife may do so. A way of promoting involvement of the husband is to have him sign the checks. If both husband and wife work, set up one bank account and have all income go into it.

Sit down and prepare a workable budget together. Establish a savings account. Determine the needs of your family and include these needs in your family budget. Present and future needs should be included. Be sure you include your tithes and offerings in your budget.

Set up separate savings accounts for vacations, college expenses, Christmas, and emergency fund. Invest your money. Set up a general ledger to easily show all checks written and all deposits made. This gives both husband and wife access and each will know what's going on with the money. Set target goals for paying off debts.

Conclusion

We have labored for the better part of a year putting our thoughts and feelings on paper on this project. We discussed the issues and researched the Bible as well as spiritual books, and any other published information we could find on blended families.

It was stressful completing this project, but we were intent on completing this project so that we could help other families. With our busy schedules, writing this book was very difficult at times. We won't bore you with all the details, but rest assured that Satan is real and he will go to any lengths to attack God's children, to be a stumbling block to stop us from doing God's will, and to have us turn away from the only One who can really help us. The more Satan came at us, the more we had to trust in God that this was what He wanted us to do.

Writing this book has served to strengthen our faith in God and our commitment to family. It is our deepest wish that if this book does nothing more than encourage just one blended family to look to God's Holy Word for the answers to their issues, we will be overwhelmingly satisfied. What we have gained from this experience is priceless.

It has strengthened our marriage, improved our relationship with each other, elevated our love for one another to a new and higher level, and it has brought our family closer together. It has also opened our eyes to things that we should have been doing but were not, and things that we were doing that we shouldn't have. We both have grown from this experience more than we could have ever imagined. We hope this book will help you achieve peace and harmony in your home.

Things were hot and cold all the time, even after giving our lives to Christ. It wasn't until the Holy Spirit began directing us that we realized what we had to do to begin to achieve the peace and harmony in our blended family that we desired. We look back now and thank God for the trials and tribulations He took us through because now our family is stronger and our marriage is better than ever. And this is what we want for everyone who is in a blended family (and, for that matter, a traditional family). We know that you too can have this fulfillment. May God bless you and be with you forever.

STOP, LOOK, LISTEN

A child whispered, "God, speak to me," and a meadowlark sang.
But the child did not hear.

So the child yelled, "God, speak to me!" And the thunder rolled across the sky.
But the child did not listen.

The child looked around and said, "God let me see you." And a star shone brightly.
But the child did not see.

And the child shouted, "God show me a miracle!" And a life was born.
But the child did not know.

So the child cried out in despair, "Touch me God, and let me know you are there!"
Whereupon God reached down And touched the child.
But the child brushed the butterfly away—
And walked off unknowingly.

Don't miss out on your blessing because it isn't packaged the way that you expect. . . .

STOP the hectic pace, LOOK more closely and LISTEN more intently.
—Anonymous

For information on ordering our Blended Family workbook or seminar leader's manual, please contact us at the address below:

The Blended Family Ministry
12138 Central Ave. PMB #672
Mitchellville, Maryland 20721
e-mail BlendFmlyMnstry@aol.com
phone: (301) 306-9448
fax: (301) 306-5187

Notes

Chapter 1

1. National Center for Health Statistics *National Vital Statistics Report: Births, Marriages, Divorces and Deaths, Provisional Data for 1998*, vol. 47, no. 21.4, pp. PHS 99–1120.

2. Kathleen Stassen Berger, *The Developing Person through the Life Span*, 4th ed. (New York: Worth Publishers, 1998), pp. 521.

3. Norval D. Glenn, "The Recent Trend in Marital Success in the United States," *Journal of Marriage and the Family*, 53 (1991): 261–270.

4. *Webster's New World Dictionary*, 2nd college ed. (New York: Simon and Schuster, Inc.), pp. 283, 1339.

5. *Women's Study Bible*, "The Creation of the Woman" (Nashville: Thomas Nelson Publishers, Inc.), p. 10.

6. Ibid., "Fall of Creation," p. 11.

7. Ibid.

8. Alan C. Acock and David H. Demo, *Family Diversity and Well Being* (Thousand Oaks, Calif.: n.p., 1994). Paul R. Sage Amato and Bruce Keith, "Parental Divorce and Adult Well Being: A Meta-analysis," *Journal of Marriage and Family* 53 (1991): pp. 43–58. Deborah A. Dawson, "Family Structure and Children's Health and Well Being: Data from the 1988 National Health Interview Study on Child Health," *Journal of Marriage and the Family* 53 (1991): pp. 573–584.

9. Berger, *The Developing Person*, pp. 367–368.

Chapter 2

1. *Women's Study Bible*, "Salvation," p. 1961.

2. Dennis Rainey, Family Life Home Builders, Couples Series, *Building Your Marriage* (Ventura Calif.: Gospel Light, 1989), p. 154.

3. Ibid., pp. 162–163.

4. *Matthew Henry's Commentary on the Whole Bible, Complete and Unabridged in One Volume* (N.p.: Hendrickson Publishers, Inc. 1991), p. 959.

Chapter 3

1. Donald Joy, *Rebonding: Preventing and Restoring Damaged Relationships* (Texas: Word Books, 1986), p. 36.

2. Martha Peace, *The Excellent Wife* (N.p.: Focus Publishing, Inc., 1999), p. 6.

3. Lonnie Collins Pratt, *Making Two Halves a Whole* (N.p.: David C. Cook Publishing Co., 1995), p. 22.

4. Larry Richards, *Remarriage: A Healing Gift from God* (Texas: Word Books, 1981), p. 46.

5. Robert J. Kastenbaum, *The Psychology of Death* (New York: Springer, 1986).

Chapter 4

1. U.S. Census Bureau Reports, 1990.

2. Berger, *The Developing Person*, p. 529.

3. Jeanne M. Tschann, "Resources, Stressors, and Attachment as Predictors of Adult Adjustment after Divorce: A Longitudinal Study," *Journal of Marriage and*

Family 51 (1989): 1033–1047.

4. Gay C. Kitson and Leslie Morgan, "The Multiple Consequences of Divorce: A Decade Review," *Journal of Marriage and the Family* 52 (1990): 913–924.

5. Berger, *The Developing Person*, p. 523.

6. Neil Anderson, *The Bondage Breaker* (Oregon: Harvest House Publishers, 1993), p. 138.

7. osl@goshen.net, Divorce, August 1999, http://www.biblestudytools.net...elicalDictionary/?word=Divorce

8. Ibid.

9. *Women's Study Bible*, p. 1583.

10. Gelles, 1993; McKenry, 1995; Oleary, 1993; Straus & Yodanis, 1996: Yllo, 1993.

Chapter 5

1. "Fruit of the Spirit," in Baker's Evangelical Dictionary of Biblical Theology.

2. *Women's Study Bible*, p. 1686.

3. Ibid., p. 949.

4. Ibid., p. 2104.

5. Ibid., p. 1889.

6. Ibid., p. 1873.

7. Ibid., p. 1910.

8. Ibid., p. 1917.

9. http://www.gospelcom.net/rbc/ds/q0504/point4.html

Chapter 6

1. National Center for Health Statistics, FASTATS, *Monthly Vital Statistics Report: Marriage* (most recent figures for U.S., 1996), vol. 45, no. 12.

2. Edith Deen, *All the Women of the Bible* (New York: Harper Collins Publishers, Inc., 1983), p. 291.

3. F. LaGard Smith, *The Narrated Bible, In Chronological Order*, New International Version (Oregon: Harvest House Publishers, 1984), p. 662.

Chapter 7

1. Paul R. Amato, "Children's Adjustment to Divorce: Theories, Hypothesis, Empirical Support," *Journal of Marriage and the Family* 53 (1993): 43–58.

2. Acock and Demo, *Family Diversity*; Amato and Keith, "Parental Divorce"; Dawson, "Family Structure," p. 366.

3. Frank F. Furstenberg Jr., and Andrew J. Cherlin, *Divided Families: What Happens to Children When Parents Part* (Cambridge, Mass.: Harvard University Press, 1991).

4. Berger, *The Developing Person*, p. 369.

5. NEB Facts, 1998.

6. Amato and Rezac, 1994.

7. Jane Hurwiz, *Coping in a Blended Family* (66), p. 71.

8. Ibid., p. 78.

9. Ibid., p. 79.

Chapter 8

1. Deen, *Women of the Bible*, p. 291.

2. American Heritage Dictionary, p. 268.

3. osl@goshen.net, Family, August 1999, http://www.biblestudytools.net...elical-Dictionary/?word=Family

4. Women's Study Bible, p. 972.

5. Donald Joy, Rebonding Preventing and Restoring Relationships, p. 81.

6. *Learning to Step Together* (Palo Alto, Calif.: Stepfamily Association of America), p. 68.

7. Pratt, *Two Halves*, 87.

8. *Women's Study Bible*

9. Webster's Dictionary, p. 1314.

10. Hurwitz, *Coping*, p. 59.

11. Hurwitz, *Coping*, p. 61.

12. *Women's Study Bible*, p. 71.

13. Emily B. Visher and John S. Visher, *Old Loyalties, New Ties: Therapeutic Strategies with Stepfamilies* (New York: Brunner/Majel, Inc., 1998), p. 19.

14. Pratt, *Two Halves*, p. 87.

15. Ibid., p. 88.

16. Henry, *Commentary*, p. 634.

Chapter 10

1. Hurwiz, *Coping*, p. 70.

2. *Training Faithful Men*, Basic Church Ministry (1984 Institute in Basic Life Principles, n.d.).

3. Ibid.